The Invention of Love

TOM STOPPARD

The Invention of Love

GROVE PRESS
New York

First published in 1997 by Faber and Faber Limited
First Grove Press edition September 1998

Printed in the United States of America

Library of Congress Cataloging-in-Publication Data

Stoppard, Tom.
    The invention of love / Tom Stoppard.
      p.   cm.
    ISBN 0-8021-3581-1
    1. Housman, A. E. (Alfred Edward), 1859–1936—Drama.   I. Title.
    PR6069.T6I66   1998
    822'.914—dc21   98-28331

Grove Press
841 Broadway
New York, NY 10003

98 99 00 01 10 9 8 7 6 5 4 3 2 1

Note to Second Edition

This text is slightly altered from the first edition in places where I have brought it into line with the performance at the Royal National Theatre. I am indebted to Richard Eyre for his patience and guidance. It is none too soon, too, to express my gratitude to two classicists, David West and Peter Jones, for unstinting kindness.

T. S.

January 1998

Characters

AEH, A. E. Housman, aged 77
Housman, A. E. Housman, aged from 18 to 26
Alfred William Pollard, aged from 18 to 26
Moses John Jackson, aged from 19 to 27
Charon, ferryman of the Underworld

In Act One:
Mark Pattison, Rector of Lincoln College, aged 64,
a classical scholar
Walter Pater, critic, essayist, scholar, fellow of Brasenose,
aged 38
John Ruskin, pre-eminent art critic, aged 58
Benjamin Jowett, Master of Balliol, aged 60
Robinson Ellis, a Latin scholar, aged 45
In addition, the Vice-Chancellor of Oxford University
and a Balliol Student

In Act Two:
Katharine Housman, sister of AEH, at the ages of
19 and 35
Henry Labouchere, Liberal MP and journalist, at the
ages of 54 and 64
Frank Harris, writer and journalist, at the ages of 29
and about 40
W. T. Stead, editor and journalist, at the ages of 36 and 46
Chamberlain, a clerk in his 20s, then 30s
John Percival Postgate, a Latin scholar, aged about 40
Jerome K. Jerome, humourist and editor, aged 38
Oscar Wilde, aged 41

In addition, **Bunthorne**, a character in *Patience* by Gilbert and Sullivan, and the **Chairman** and **Members of the Selection Committee**

The two groups of characters appearing only in Act One or Act Two, respectively, may be played by the same group of actors.
References in the stage directions to river, boats, garden, etc., need not be taken at face value.

The **Invention of Love** opened at the Cottesloe Theatre,
Royal National Theatre, London, on 25 September 1997
with the following cast:

AEH John Wood
Charon Michael Bryant
Housman Paul Rhys
Pollard Stephen Mapes
Jackson Robert Portal
The Vice-Chancellor of Oxford University William Chubb
Pattison William Chubb
Pater Robin Soans
A Balliol Student Ben Porter
Jowett John Carlisle
Ruskin Benjamin Whitrow
Ellis Paul Benzing
Katharine Emma Dewhurst
Bunthorne Michael Fitzgerald
Labouchere Benjamin Whitrow
Harris Robin Soans
Stead John Carlisle
Chamberlain Ben Porter
Chairman of Selection Committee Michael Bryant
Member of Selection Committee Paul Benzing
Postgate William Chubb
Jerome Paul Benzing
Wilde Michael Fitzgerald

Directed by Richard Eyre
Designed by Anthony Ward
Lighting by Peter Mumford

Act One

AEH, aged seventy-seven and getting no older, wearing a buttoned-up dark suit and neat black boots, stands on the bank of the Styx watching the approach of the ferryman, Charon.

AEH I'm dead, then. Good. And this is the Stygian gloom one has heard so much about.

Charon Belay the painter there, sir!

AEH 'Belay the painter!' The tongues of men and of angels!

Charon See the cleat. I trust you had grieving friends and family, sir, to give you a decent burial.

AEH Cremation, but very decent I believe: a service at Trinity College and the ashes laid to rest – for fathomable reasons – in Shropshire, a county where I never lived and seldom set foot.

Charon So long as the wolves and bears don't dig you up.

AEH No fear of that. The jackals are another matter. One used to say, 'After I'm dead'. The consolation is not as complete as one had supposed. There – the painter is belayed. I heard Ruskin lecture in my first term at Oxford. Painters belayed on every side. He died mad. As you may have noticed. Are we waiting for someone?

Charon He's late. I hope nothing's happened to him. What do they call you, sir?

AEH Alfred Housman is my name. My friends call me Housman. My enemies call me Professor Housman. Now you're going to ask me for a coin, and, regrettably, the custom of putting a coin in the mouth of the deceased is foreign to the Evelyn Nursing Home and probably against the rules. (*looking out*) Doubly late. Are you sure?

Charon A poet and a scholar is what I was told.

AEH I think that must be me.

Charon Both of them?

AEH I'm afraid so.

Charon It sounded like two different people.

AEH I know.

Charon Give him a minute.

AEH To collect myself. Ah, look, I've found a sixpence. Mint. 1936 Anno Domini.

Charon You know Latin.

AEH I should say I do. I am – I was, for twenty-five years, Benjamin Hall Kennedy Professor of Latin at Cambridge. Is Kennedy here? I should like to meet him.

Charon Everyone is here, and those that aren't will be. Sit in the middle.

AEH Of course. Well, I don't suppose I'll have time to meet everybody.

Charon Yes, you will, but Benjamin Hall Kennedy isn't usually first choice.

AEH I didn't mean to suggest that he is mine. He imputed to the practice of translation into Greek and Latin verse a value which it does not really possess, at least not as an insight into the principles of ancient metre.

It stands to reason that you are not likely to discover the laws of metre by composing verses in which you occasionally break those laws because you have not yet discovered them. But Kennedy was a schoolmaster, a schoolmaster of genius but a schoolmaster. It was only in an outbreak of sentimentality that Cambridge named a chair after him. I would have countenanced a small inkpot. Even so, let it be said, it is to Kennedy, or more directly to his *Sabrinae Corolla*, the third edition, which I received as a school prize when I was seventeen, that I owe my love of Latin and Greek. In Greek I am, as it were, an amateur, and know hardly more than the professors: well, a great deal more than Pearson, who knew more than Jowett and Jebb (knew) combined. As Regius Professor of Greek when I was at Oxford, Jowett was contaminated by a misplaced enthusiasm for classical education, which to him meant supplying the governing classes with Balliol men who had read some Plato, or with Oxford men who had read some Plato when Balliol men who had read some Plato were not available. In my first week, which was in October 1877, I heard Jowett pronounce '*akribos*' with the accent on the first syllable, and I thought, 'Well! So much for Jowett!' With Jebb it was Sophocles. There are places in Jebb's Sophocles where the responsibility for reading the metre seems to have been handed over to the Gas, Light and Coke Company.

Charon Could you keep quiet for a bit?

AEH Yes, I expect so. My life was marked by long silences.

Charon unties the painter and starts to pole.

Who *is* usually first choice?

Charon Helen of Troy. You'll see a three-headed dog

when we've crossed over. If you don't take any notice of him he won't take any notice of you.

Voices off-stage – yapping dog, splashing oars.

Housman . . . yea, we have been forsaken in the wilderness to gather grapes of thorns and figs of thistles!

Pollard Pull on your right, Jackson.

Jackson Do you want to take the oars?

Pollard No, you're doing splendidly.

Three men in a boat row into view, small dog yapping. Housman in the bow (holding the dog), Jackson rowing, Pollard in the stern. The dog is played realistically by a toy (stuffed) dog.

Jackson Hous hasn't done any work since Iffley.

AEH Mo!

Housman The nerve of it – who brought you up from Hades? – to say nothing of the dog.

Pollard The dog says nothing of you. The dog loves Jackson.

Housman Jackson loves the dog.

Pollard The uninflected dog the uninflected Jackson loves, that's the beauty of it. Good dog.

Housman The uninflected dog can't be good, dogs have no soul.

Jackson What did he say?

Pollard He said your dog has no soul.

Jackson What a cheek!

Pollard It just goes to show you don't know much about

4

dogs, and nothing at all about Jackson's dog whose soul is already bespoke for the Elysian Fields, where it is eagerly awaited by many of his friends who are not gone but only sleeping.

AEH Not dead, only dreaming!

The three men row out of view, arguing 'Pull on your right!' . . . 'Is anybody hungry?'

Charon Well, I never! Brought their own boat, whatever next?

AEH I had only to stretch out my hand! – *ripae ulterioris amore!* (*cries out*) Oh, Mo! Mo! I would have died for you but I never had the luck!

Charon The dog?

AEH My greatest friend and comrade Moses Jackson. '*Nec Lethaea valet Theseus abrumpere caro vincula Pirithoo.*'

Charon That's right, I remember him – Theseus – trying to break the chains that held fast his friend, to take him back with him from the Underworld. But it can't be done, sir. It can't be done.

Charon poles the ferry into the mist.
Light on Vice-Chancellor in robes of office. His voice is echoing. Alternatively, he is heard only.

Vice-Chancellor Alfredus Edvardus Housman.

Housman, aged eighteen, comes forward and receives a 'book' from him.

Alfredus Guilielmus Pollard . . . Moses Johannus Jackson . . .

Light on Pollard, eighteen, and Jackson, nineteen, with their statute books.

5

Jackson What is '*trochum*'?

Pollard A hoop, in the accusative.

Jackson '*Neque volvere . . .*'

Pollard Yes, we are forbidden by the statutes to trundle a hoop. I'm Pollard. I believe we have the two open scholarships this year. May I offer my congratulations.

Jackson How do you do? Well, congratulations to you, too.

Pollard Where were you at school?

Jackson The Vale Academy. It's in Ramsgate. Actually my father is the Principal. But I haven't come from school, I've been two years at University College, London. I did a bit of rowing there, actually. And you?

Pollard King's College School.

Jackson You play rugby, don't you?

Pollard Yes. Not personally.

Jackson I prefer rugby football to Association rules. I wonder if the College turns out a strong side. I don't count myself a serious cricketer though I can put in a useful knock on occasion. Field athletics is probably what I'll concentrate on in the Easter term.

Pollard Ah. So long as it's not trundling a hoop.

Jackson No, I'm a runner first and foremost, I suppose. The quarter-mile and the half-mile are my best distances.

Pollard So you're keen on sport.

Jackson One is at Oxford to work, of course, but as the poet said – all work and no play . . .

Pollard (*overlapping*) *Orandum est ut sit mens sana in corpore sano.*

Jackson . . . makes Jack a dull boy.

Pollard I didn't realize that the classics scholarship was open to university men.

Jackson Classics? No, that's not me. I have the science scholarship.

Pollard (*happily*) Oh . . . *Science*! Sorry! How do you do?

Jackson I'm Jackson.

Pollard Pollard. Congratulations. That explains it.

Jackson What?

Pollard I don't know. Yes, *trochus* comes into Ovid, or Horace somewhere, the *Satires*.

   Housman joins.

Housman The *Odes*. Sorry. *Odes Three*, 24, '*ludere doctior seu Graeco iubeas trocho*' – it's where he's saying everything's gone to the dogs.

Pollard That's it! Highborn young men can't sit on a horse and are afraid to hunt, they're better at playing with the Greek hoop!

Housman Actually, '*trochos*' *is* Greek, it's the Greek word for hoop, so when Horace uses '*Graecus trochus*' it's rather like saying 'French *chapeau*'. I mean he's laying it on thick, isn't he?

Jackson Is he? What?

Housman Well, to a Roman, to call something *Greek* meant – very often – sissylike, or effeminate. In fact, a hoop, a *trochos*, was a favourite gift given by a Greek man to the boy he, you know, to his favourite boy.

Jackson Oh, beastliness, you mean?

7

Pollard This is Mr Jackson, by the way.

Housman How do you do, sir?

Jackson I say, I'm a freshman too, you know. Have you seen there's a board where you put your name down? I'm going to try for the Torpids next term. Perhaps I'll see you at the river.

Pollard (*overlapping*) – at dinner – *river*.

Jackson goes.

A science scholar.

Housman Seems quite decent, though.

Pollard I'm Pollard.

Housman Housman. We're on the same staircase.

Pollard Oh, spiffing. Where were you at school?

Housman Bromsgrove. It's in, well, Bromsgrove, in fact. It's a place in Worcestershire.

Pollard I was at King's College School – that's in London.

Housman I've been to London. I went to the Albert Hall and the British Museum. The best thing was the Guards, though. You were right about Ovid, by the way. *Trochus* is in *Ars. Am.*

An Oxford garden, a river, a garden seat.
An invisible 'croquet ball' rolls on, followed by Pattison with a croquet mallet.

Pattison My young friends, I am very grieved to tell you that if you have come up to Oxford with the idea of getting knowledge, you must give that up at once. We have bought you, and we're running you in two plates, Mods and the Finals.

Pollard Yes, sir.

Pattison The curriculum is designed on the idle plan that all of knowledge will be found inside the covers of four Latin and four Greek books, though not the same four each year.

Housman Thank you, sir.

Pattison A genuine love of learning is one of the two delinquencies which cause blindness and lead a young man to ruin.

Pollard/Housman (*leaving*) Yes, sir, thank you, sir.

Pattison Hopeless.

Pattison knocks his croquet ball off-stage and follows it.
    Pater enters attended by a Balliol Student. The Student is handsome and debonair. Pater is short, unhandsome, a dandy: top hat, yellow gloves, blue cravat.

Pater Thank you for sending me your sonnet, dear boy. And also for your photograph, of course. But why do you always write poetry? Why don't you write prose? Prose is so much more difficult.

Student No one has written the poetry I wish to write, Mr Pater, but you have already written the prose.

Pater That is charmingly said. I will look at your photograph more carefully when I get home.

They leave.
    Ruskin and Jowett enter, playing croquet.

Ruskin I was seventeen when I came up to Oxford. That was in 1836, and the word 'Aesthete' was unknown. Aesthetics was newly arrived from Germany but there was no suggestion that it involved dressing up, as it might be the London Fire Brigade; nor that it was connected in some way with that excessive admiration for male physical beauty which conduced to the fall of Greece. It was not until the 1860s that moral degeneracy came under the baleful protection of artistic licence and advertised itself as aesthetic. Before that, unnatural behaviour was generally left behind at school, like football . . .

Jowett Alas, I was considered very beautiful at school. I had golden curls. The other boys called me Miss Jowett. How I dreaded that ghastly ritual! – the torment! – the humiliation! – my body ached from the indignities, I used to run away whenever the ball came near me . . .

As they leave.

No one now, I think, calls me Miss Jowett . . . or Mistress of Balliol.

Housman, Pollard and Jackson enter in a boat, Jackson rowing.

Housman False quantities in all around I see, yea we have been forsaken in the wilderness to gather grapes of thorns and figs of thistles.

Pollard That's possibly why the College is named for John the Baptist.

Jackson John the Baptist was locusts and wild honey, actually, Pollard.

Pollard It's the Baptist School of Hard Knocks. First the Wilderness, then the head on the platter.

Housman It was clear something was amiss from the day we matriculated. The statutes warned us against drinking, gambling and hoop-trundling but not a word about Jowett's translation of Plato. The Regius Professor can't even pronounce the Greek language and there is no one at Oxford to tell him.

Pollard Except you, Housman.

Housman I will take his secret to the grave, telling people I meet on the way. Betrayal is no sin if it's whimsical.

Jackson We did the new pronunciation, you know. As an Englishman I never took to the speaking of it. *Veni, vidi, vici* . . . It was never natural to my mind.

Latin pronunciation: 'wayny, weedy, weeky'.

Pollard That was Latin, actually, Jackson.

Jackson And 'Wennus' the Goddess of Love. I mean to say!

Pollard Perhaps I don't make myself plain. Latin and Greek are two entirely separate languages spoken by distinct peoples living in different parts of the ancient world. Some inkling of this must have got through to you, Jackson, at the Vale Academy, Ramsgate, surely.

Housman But '"Wennus" the Goddess of Love', for a man of Jackson's venereal pursuits, is a strong objection to the new pronunciation – where is the chemistry in Wennus?

Jackson I know you and Pollard look down on science.

Pollard Is it a science? Ovid said it was an art.

Jackson Oh – *love*! You're just ragging me because you've never kissed a girl.

Pollard Well, what's it like, Jackson?

Jackson Kissing girls is not like science, nor is it like sport. It is the third thing when you thought there were only two.

Pollard Gosh.

Housman *Da mi basia mille, deinde centum.*

Pollard Catullus! Give me a thousand kisses, and then a hundred! Then another thousand, then a second hundred! – yes, Catullus is Jackson's sort of poet.

Jackson How does it go? Is it suitable for sending to Miss Liddell as my own work?

Pollard That depends on which Miss Liddell. Does she go dum-di-di?

Jackson I very much doubt it. She's the daughter of the Dean of Christ Church.

Pollard You misunderstand. She has to scan with Lesbia. All Catullus's love poems are written to Lesbia, or about her. '*Vivamus, mea Lesbia, atque amemus . . .*'

Jackson I mean in English. Girls who kiss don't know Latin.

Pollard Oh, in English. Come on, Housman. 'Let us live, my Lesbia, and let us love, and value at one penny the murmurs of disapproving old men . . .'

Housman 'And not give tuppence for the mutterence of old men's tut-tutterence.'

Pollard He's such a show-off.

Housman
'Suns can set and rise again: when our brief light
is gone we sleep the sleep of perpetual night.
Give me a thousand kisses, and then a hundred more,
and then another thousand, and add five score . . .'

Jackson But what happens in the end?

Housman In the end they're both dead and Catullus is set for Moderations. *Nox est perpetua.*

Pollard It's not perpetual if he's set for Mods.

Housman Is that Church of England?

Jackson Did they get married?

Pollard No. They loved, and quarrelled, and made up, and loved, and fought, and were true to each other and untrue. She made him the happiest man in the whole world and the most wretched, and after a few years she died, and then, when he was thirty, he died, too. But by that time Catullus had invented the love poem.

Jackson He *invented* it? Did he, Hous?

Pollard You don't have to ask *him*. Like everything else, like clocks and trousers and algebra, the love poem had to be invented. After millenniums of sex and centuries of poetry, the love poem as understood by Shakespeare and Donne, and by Oxford undergraduates – the true-life confessions of the poet in love, immortalizing the mistress, who is actually *the cause of the poem – that* was invented in Rome in the first century before Christ.

Jackson Gosh.

Housman *Basium* is a point of interest. A kiss was always *osculum* until Catullus.

Pollard Now, Hous, concentrate – is that the point of interest in the kiss?

Housman Yes.

Pollard Pull on your right.

Jackson Do you want to take the oars?

Pollard No, you're doing splendidly.

Jackson Hous hasn't done any work since below Iffley.

Housman The nerve of it! Who brought us up from Hades?

They row out of sight.
  The croquet game returns – Pattison, followed in series by Jowett, Pater and Ruskin. The game accounts for the entrances, actions and exits of Pattison, Pater, Jowett and Ruskin.

Pattison I was not quite seventeen when I first saw Oxford. That was in 1830 and Oxford was delightful then, not the overbuilt slum it has become. The town teems with people who have no business here, which is to say business is all they have. The University held off the London and Birmingham Railway until the forties, and I said at the time, 'If the Birmingham train comes, can the London train be far behind?'

Pater I don't think that can be quite right, Dr Pattison.

Jowett Posting ten miles to Steventon for the Paddington train was never anything to cherish. Personally, I thank God for the branch line, and hope His merciful bounty is not exhausted by changing at Didcot.

Ruskin When I am at Paddington I feel I am in hell.

Jowett You must not go about telling everyone, Dr Ruskin. It will not do for the moral education of Oxford undergraduates that the wages of sin may be no more than the sense of being stranded at one of the larger railway stations.

Ruskin To be morally educated is to realize that such would be a terrible price. Mechanical advance is the slack taken up of our failing humanity. Hell is very likely to be modernization infinitely extended. There is a rocky valley between Buxton and Bakewell where once you may have seen at first and last light the Muses dance for Apollo and heard the pan-pipes play. But its rocks were blasted away for the railway, and now every fool in Buxton can be at Bakewell in half an hour, and every fool in Bakewell at Buxton.

Pater (*at croquet*) First-class return.

Jowett Mind the gap.

Pattison Personally I am in favour of education but a university is not the place for it. A university exists to seek the meaning of life by the pursuit of scholarship.

Ruskin I have announced the meaning of life in my lectures. There is nothing beautiful which is not good, and nothing good which has no moral purpose. I had my students up at dawn building a flower-bordered road across a swamp at Ferry Hinksey. There was an Irish exquisite, a great slab of a youth with white hands and long poetical hair who said he was glad to say he had never seen a shovel, but I made him a navvy for one term and taught him that the work of one's hands is the beginning of virtue. Then I went sketching to Venice and the road sank into the swamp. My protégé rose at noon to smoke cigarettes and read French novels, and Oxford reverted to a cockney watering-place for learning to row.

Housman and Pollard enter along the river bank,
Housman intent on an unseen boat race.

Housman Come on, St John's!

Pollard Ruskin said, when he's at Paddington he feels he is in hell – and this man Oscar Wilde said, 'Ah, but –'

Housman '– when he's in hell he'll think he's only at Paddington.' It'll be a pity if inversion is all he is known for. Row up, St John's!

Pollard You *hate* sport.

Housman Keep the stroke!

15

Pollard Wilde is reckoned the wittiest man at Oxford. His rooms at Magdalen are said to be completely bare except for a lily in a blue vase.

Housman No furniture?

Pollard Well, of course there is *furniture* . . . I suppose there is furniture.

Housman Come on, St John's!

Pollard He went to the Morrell's ball in a Prince Rupert costume which he has absentmindedly put on every morning since, and has been seen wearing it in the High. Everyone is repeating his remark that he finds it harder and harder every day to live up to his blue china. Don't you think that's priceless?

Housman We have a blue china butterdish at Bromsgrove, we never take any notice of it.
    Well rowed! Bad luck, St John's!

Jowett I was eighteen when I came up to Oxford. That was in 1835, and Oxford was an utter disgrace. Education rarely interfered with the life of the University. Learning was carried on in nooks and corners, like Papism in an Elizabethan manor house. The fellows were socially negligible, and perfectly astonished by the historical process that had placed the teaching of undergraduates into the hands of amiable clergymen waiting for preferment to a country parsonage. I say nothing against the undergraduates, a debauched and indolent rabble as it happens. The great reform of the fifties laid the foundation of the educated class that has spread moral and social order to parts of the world where, to take one example, my Plato was formerly quite unknown.

Pattison The great reform made us into a cramming shop. The railway brings in the fools and takes them away with their tickets punched for the world outside.

Jowett The modern university exists by consent of the world outside. We must send out men fitted for that world. What better example can we show them than classical antiquity? Nowhere was the ideal of morality, art and social order realized more harmoniously than in Greece in the age of the great philosophers.

Ruskin Buggery apart.

Jowett Buggery apart.

Pater Actually, Italy in the late-fifteenth century . . . Nowhere was the ideal of art, morality and social order realized more harmoniously, morality and social order apart.

Ruskin The Medieval Gothic! The Medieval Gothic cathedrals which were the great engines of art, morality and social order!

Pattison (*at croquet*) Check. Play the advantage.

Pater I have been touched by the medieval but its moment has passed, and now I wouldn't return the compliment with a barge-pole. As for arts-and-crafts, it is very well for the people; without it, Liberty's would be at risk, in fact it would be closed, but the true Aesthetic spirit goes back to Florence, Venice, Rome – Japanese apart. One sees it plain in Michelangelo's *David* – legs apart.* The blue of my very necktie declares that we are still living in that revolution whereby man regained possession of his nature and produced the Italian Tumescence.

Pattison Renaissance, surely. Deuce.

Pater On the frescoed walls of Santa Maria della Grazie

*For this deplorable image the author gratefully acknowledges the actor playing Pater, Robin Soans.

and the painted ceiling of St Pancras –

Pattison Peter's, surely. Leg-before unless I'm much mistaken.

Jackson comes, in rowing kit.

Housman Well rowed, Jackson! I'm afraid they had the measure of us.

Jackson Extraordinary thing. Fellow in velvet knickerbockers like something from the halls came up and said he wished to compliment me on my race. I replied with dignity, 'Thank you, but although my first name happens to be Moses I am not Jewish and can take no merit from it.' He said, 'Allow me to do the jokes, it's what I'm at Oxford for – I saw you in the Torpids and your left leg is a poem.'

Pollard What did you say?

Jackson Naturally, I asked him if he was a rowing man. He said he tried out for an oar in the Magdalen boat but couldn't see the use of going backwards down to Iffley every evening so he gave it up and now plays no outdoor games at all, except dominoes: he has sometimes played dominoes outside French cafés. Do you know what I think he is?

Pollard What?

Jackson I think he's one of those Aesthetes.

They go.

Ruskin Conscience, faith, disciplined restraint, fidelity to nature – all the Christian virtues that gave us the cathedral at Chartres, the paintings of Giotto, the poetry of Dante – have been tricked out in iridescent rags to catch the attention of the moment.

Pater In the young Raphael, in the sonnets of
Michelangelo, in Correggio's lily-bearer in the cathedral
at Parma, and ever so faintly in my necktie, we feel the
touch of a, what shall I say? –

Pattison Barge-pole?

Pater Barge-pole? . . . No . . . the touch of a refined and
comely paganism that rescued beauty from the charnel
house of the Christian conscience. The Renaissance
teaches us that the book of knowledge is not to be learned
by rote but is to be written anew in the ecstasy of living
each moment for the moment's sake. Success in life is to
maintain this ecstasy, to burn always with this hard gem-
like flame. Failure is to form habits. To burn with a gem-
like flame is to capture the awareness of each moment;
and for that moment only. To form habits is to be absent
from those moments. How may we always be present for
them? – to garner not the fruits of experience but experience itself? –

*At a distance, getting no closer, Jackson is seen as a run-
ner running towards us.*
The game takes Ruskin and Pattison out.

. . . to catch at the exquisite passion, the strange flower, or
art – or the face of one's friend? For, not to do so in our
short day of frost and sun is to sleep before evening. The
conventional morality which requires of us the sacrifice of
any one of those moments has no real claim on us. The
love of art for art's sake seeks nothing in return except the
highest quality to the moments of your life, and simply
for those moments' sake.

Jowett Mr Pater, can you spare a moment?

Pater Certainly! As many as you like!

Jackson arrives out of breath. Housman meets him,

19

holding a watch. Jackson sits exhausted on the seat. Housman has a home-made 'laurel crown'. He crowns Jackson – a lighthearted gesture.

Housman One minute, fifty-eight seconds.

Jackson What . . .?

Housman One fifty-eight, exactly.

Jackson That's nonsense.

Housman Or two fifty-eight.

Jackson That's nonsense the other way. What was the first quarter?

Housman I'm afraid I forgot to look.

Jackson What were you doing?

Housman Watching you.

Jackson You duffer!

Housman Why can't it be one fifty-eight?

Jackson The world record for the half is over two minutes.

Housman Oh, well . . . congratulations, Jackson.

Jackson What will become of you, Hous?

Jackson takes off the laurel and leaves it on the seat, as he leaves. Housman picks up the book.

Housman It has become of me.

Pater The story has been grossly exaggerated, it has, if you will, accrued grossness in the telling, but when all's said and done, a letter signed 'Yours lovingly' –

Jowett Several letters, and addressed to an undergraduate.

Pater Several letters signed 'Yours lovingly' and addressed to an undergraduate –

Jowett Of Balliol.

Pater Even of Balliol, do not prove beastliness – would hardly support a suggestion of spooniness, in fact –

Jowett From a *tutor*, sir, a fellow not even of his own College, thanking him for a *disgusting sonnet!*

Pater You feel, in short, Dr Jowett, that I have overstepped the mark.

Jowett I feel, Mr Pater, that letters to an undergraduate signed 'Yours lovingly', thanking him for a sonnet on the honeyed mouth and lissome thighs of Ganymede, would be capable of a construction fatal to the ideals of higher learning even if the undergraduate in question were not colloquially known as the Balliol bugger.

Pater You astonish me.

Jowett The Balliol bugger, I am assured.

Pater No, no, I am astonished that you should take exception to an obviously Platonic enthusiasm.

Jowett A Platonic enthusiasm as far as Plato was concerned meant an enthusiasm of the kind that would empty the public schools and fill the prisons where it is not nipped in the bud. In my translation of the Phaedrus it required all my ingenuity to rephrase his depiction of paederastia into the affectionate regard as exists between an Englishman and his wife. Plato would have made the transposition himself if he had had the good fortune to be a Balliol man.

Pater And yet, Master, no amount of ingenuity can dispose of boy-love as the distinguishing feature of a society which we venerate as one of the most brilliant in the history of human culture, raised far above its neighbours in moral and mental distinction.

Jowett You are very kind but one undergraduate is hardly a distinguishing feature, and I have written to his father to remove him. (*to Housman, who is arriving with a new book*) Pack your bags, sir, and be gone! The canker that brought low the glory that was Greece shall not prevail over Balliol!

Pater (*leaving, to Housman*) It's a long story, but there is a wash and it will all come out in it.

Housman I am Housman, sir, of St John's.

Jowett Then I am at a loss to understand why I should be addressing you. Who is your tutor?

Housman I go to Mr Warren at Magdalen three times a week.

Jowett That must be it. Warren is a Balliol man, he has spoken of you, he believes you capable of great things.

Housman Really, sir?

Jowett If you can rid yourself of your levity and your cynicism, and find another way to dissimulate your Irish provincialism than by making affected remarks about your blue china and going about in plum-coloured velvet breeches, which you don't, and cut your hair – you're not him at all, are you? Never mind, what have you got there? Oh, Munro's *Catullus*. I glanced at it in Blackwell's. A great deal of Munro and precious little of Catullus. It's amazing what people will pay four shillings and sixpence for. Is Catullus on your reading list?

Housman Yes, sir, 'The Marriage of Peleus and Thetis'.

Jowett Catullus 64! Lord Leighton should paint that opening scene! The flower of the young men of Argos hot

for the capture of the Golden Fleece, churning the waves
with their blades of pine, the first ship ever to plough the
ocean! 'And the wild faces of the sea-nymphs emerged
from the white foaming waters – *emersere feri candenti e
gurgite vultus aequoreae* – staring in amazement at the
sight – *monstrum Nereides admirantes.*'

Housman Yes, sir. *Freti*, actually, sir.

Jowett What?

Housman Munro concurs that *feri* is a mistake for *freti*,
sir, because *vultus* must be accusative.

Jowett Concurs with whom?

Housman Concurs with, well, everybody.

Jowett Everybody but Catullus. The textual critics have
spoken. Death to wild faces emerging in the nominative.
Long live the transitive *emersere* raising up the accusative
unqualified faces from the white foaming waters, of the
freti, something watery like channel. Never mind that we
already have so many watery words that the last thing we
need is another – here we are: '*freti* for *feri* is an easy cor-
rection, as r, t, tr, rt are among the letters most frequently
confounded in the manuscripts.' Well, Munro is entitled
to concur with everybody who amends the manuscripts of
Catullus according to his taste and calls his taste his conjectures – it's a futile business suitable to occupy the
leisure of professors of Cambridge University. But you, sir,
have not been put on earth with an Oxford scholarship so
that you may bother your head with whether Catullus in
such-and-such place wrote *ut* or *et* or *aut* or none of them
or whether such-and-such line is spurious or corrupt or
on the contrary an example of Catullus's peculiar genius.
You are here to take the ancient authors as they come
from a reputable English printer, and to study them until
you can write in the metre. If you cannot write Latin and

Greek verse how can you hope to be of any use in the world?

Housman But isn't it of use to establish what the ancient authors really wrote?

Jowett It would be on the whole desirable rather than undesirable and the job was pretty well done, where it could be done, by good scholars dead these hundred years and more. For the rest, certainty could only come from recovering the autograph. This morning I had cause to have typewritten an autograph letter I wrote to the father of a certain undergraduate. The copy as I received it asserted that the Master of Balliol had a solemn duty to stamp out unnatural mice. In other words, anyone with a secretary knows that what Catullus really wrote was already corrupt by the time it was copied twice, which was about the time of the first Roman invasion of Britain: and the earliest copy that has come down to *us* was written about 1,500 years after that. Think of all those secretaries! – corruption breeding corruption from papyrus to papyrus, and from the last disintegrating scrolls to the first new-fangled parchment books, with a thousand years of copying-out still to come, running the gauntlet of changing forms of script and spelling, and absence of punctuation – not to mention mildew and rats and fire and flood and Christian disapproval to the brink of extinction as what Catullus really wrote passed from scribe to scribe, this one drunk, that one sleepy, another without scruple, and of those sober, wide-awake and scrupulous, some ignorant of Latin and some, even worse, fancying themselves better Latinists than Catullus – until! – finally and at long last – mangled and tattered like a dog that has fought its way home, there falls across the threshold of the Italian Renaissance the sole surviving witness to thirty generations of carelessness and stupidity: the *Verona Codex* of Catullus; which was almost immediately lost again, but not before being copied with one last opportunity for error. And there you have the foundation of the poems of Catullus as they went to the printer for the first time, in Venice 400 years ago.

Housman Where, sir?

Jowett (*pointing*) In there.

Housman Do you mean, sir, that it's here in Oxford?

Jowett Why, yes. That is why it is called the *Codex Oxoniensis*. Only recently was its importance recognized, by a German scholar who made the *Oxoniensis* the foundation of his edition of the poet. Mr Robinson Ellis of Trinity College discovered its existence several years before but, unluckily, not its importance, and *his* edition of Catullus has the singular distinction of vitiating itself by ignoring the discovery of its own editor.

Ellis enters as a child with a lollipop, on a scooter; but not dressed as a child.

Awfully hard cheese, Ellis! Ignoring your *Oxoniensis*!

Ellis Didn't ignore it.

Jowett Did.

Ellis Didn't.

Jowett Did.

Ellis Didn't!

They continue thuswise as AEH and Charon pole into view on the river.

Jowett Did.

Ellis Didn't.

Jowett (*leaving*) Did, did, did!

Ellis Didn't! And anyway, Baehrens overvalued it, so there!

AEH That's Bobby Ellis! He's somewhat altered in demeanour, but the intellect is unmistakable.

Ellis Young man, they tell me you are an absolutely safe First. I am proposing to form a class next term to read the Monobiblos. The fee will be one pound.

Housman The Monobiblos?

AEH I've seen *him* before, too.

Ellis Dear me. Propertius Book One.

Housman Propertius.

Ellis The greatest of the Roman love elegists, and the most corrupt.

Housman Oh.

Ellis Only Catullus has a later text, but I would say Propertius is the more corrupt.

Housman Oh – *corrupt*. Yes. Thank you, sir.

They go.

AEH Do you know Propertius?

Charon You mean personally?

AEH I mean the poems.

Charon Ah. No, then. Here we are. Elysium.

AEH Elysium! Where else?! I was eighteen when I first saw Oxford, and Oxford was charming then, not the trippery emporium it has become. There were horse-buses at the station to meet the Birmingham train; and not a brick to be seen, before the Kinema and Kardomah. The Oxford of my dreams, re-dreamt. The desire to urinate,

26

combined with a sense that it would not be a good idea, usually means we are asleep.

Charon Or in a boat. That happened to me once.

AEH Were you asleep?

Charon No, I was in a play.

AEH That needs thinking about.

Charon Aristophanes, *The Frogs*.

AEH You speak the truth. I saw you.

Charon I had that Dionysus in the back of my boat.

AEH You were very good.

Charon No, I was just in it. I was caught short. Good stuff, *The Frogs*, don't you think?

AEH Not particularly. But it quotes from Aeschylus.

Charon Ah, now that was a play.

AEH What was?

Charon Aeschylus, *Myrmidones*. Do you know it?

AEH It didn't survive; only the title and some fragments. I would join Sisyphus in Hades and gladly push my boulder up the slope if only, each time it rolled back down, I were given a line of Aeschylus.

Charon I think I can remember some of it.

AEH Oh my goodness.

Charon Give me a minute.

AEH Oh my Lord.

Charon Achilles is in his tent.

AEH Oh please don't let it be a dream!

Charon The chorus is his clansmen, the Myrmidons.

AEH Yes.

Charon They tell him off for sulking in his –

AEH Tent, yes, but can you remember an actual line that Aeschylus *wrote*?

Charon I'm coming to it. First Achilles compares himself to an eagle hit by an arrow fledged with one of its own feathers, do you know that one?

AEH The words, the words.

Charon Achilles is in his –

AEH Tent.

Charon Tent – am I telling this or are you? – he's playing dice with himself when news comes that Patroclus has been killed. Achilles goes mad, blaming him, you see, for being dead. Now for the line. 'Does it mean nothing to you,' he says, 'the unblemished thighs I worshipped and the showers of kisses you had from me.'

AEH
σέβας δὲ μηρῶν ἁγνὸν οὐκ ἐπηδέσω,
ὦ δυσχάριστε τῶν πυκνῶν φιλημάτων.

Charon There you go.

AEH Yes, I see.

Charon No good?

AEH Very good. It's one of the fragments that has come down to us. Also the metaphor of the eagle, but not Aeschylus's own words, which I dare say you can't recall.

Charon It's maddening, isn't it?

AEH Quite so. All is plain. I may as well wet the bed, the night nurse will change the sheets and tuck me up without reproach. They are very kind to me here in the Evelyn Nursing Home.

Jackson (*off-stage*) Housman!

Pollard (*off-stage*) Housman!

Charon Look alive, then! Get it?

AEH Indeed yes.

Charon I've got dozens of them like that.

AEH Perhaps next time.

Charon I'm afraid not.

AEH Ah yes. Where is thy sting?

Charon poles AEH to the shore.

Pollard (*off-stage*) Hous! – Picnic!

Jackson (*off-stage*) Locusts! Honey!

Housman enters with a pile of books which he puts down on the seat.

Housman I say, can I give you a hand?

AEH (*to Charon*) Who's that?

Charon Who's that, he says.

AEH (*to Housman*) Thank you!

Charon Dead on time.

Housman helps AEH ashore.

AEH Most opportune.

Charon Dead on time! – there's no end to them! (*He poles himself away.*)

AEH Don't mind him. What are you doing here, may one ask?

Housman Classics, sir. I'm studying for Greats.

AEH Are you? I did Greats, too. Of course, that was more than fifty years ago, when Oxford was still the sweet city of dreaming spires.

Housman It must have been delightful then.

AEH It was. I felt as if I had come up from the plains of Moab to the top of Mount Pisgah like Moses when the Lord showed him all the land of Judah unto the utmost sea.

Housman There's a hill near our house where I live in Worcestershire which I and my brothers and sisters call Mount Pisgah. I used to climb it often, and look out towards Wales, to what I thought was a kind of Promised Land, though it was only the Clee Hills really – Shropshire was our western horizon.

AEH Oh . . . excellent. You are . . .

Housman Housman, sir, of St John's.

AEH Well, this is an unexpected development. Where can we sit down before philosophy finds us out. I'm not as young as I was. Whereas you, of course, are.

They sit.

Classical studies, eh?

Housman Yes, sir.

AEH You are to be a rounded man, fit for the world, a man of taste and moral sense.

Housman Yes, sir.

AEH Science for our material improvement, classics for

our inner nature. The beautiful and the good. Culture. Virtue. The ideas and moral influence of the ancient philosophers.

Housman Yes, sir.

AEH Humbug.

Housman Oh.

AEH Looking about you, does it appear to you that the classical fellows are the superior in sense, morality, taste, or even amiability, to the scientists?

Housman I'm acquainted with only one person in the Science School, and he is the finest man I know.

AEH And he knows more than the ancient philosophers.

Housman (Oh – !)

AEH They made the best use of the knowledge they had. They were the best minds. The French are the best cooks, and during the Siege of Paris I'm sure rats never tasted better, but that is no reason to continue eating rat now that *coq au vin* is available. The only reason to consider what the ancient philosophers meant about anything is if it's relevant to settling corrupt or disputed passages in the text. With the poets there may be other reasons for reading them; I wouldn't discount it – it may even improve your inner nature, if the miraculous collusion of sound and sense in, let us say, certain poems by Horace, teaches humility in regard to adding to the store of available literature poems by, let us say, yourself. But the effect is not widespread. Are these your books?

Housman Yes, sir.

AEH What have we here? (*He looks at Housman's books, reading the spines. He never opens them.*) Propertius! And . . . Propertius! And, of course, Propertius.

Housman (*eagerly*) Do you know him?

AEH No, not as yet.

Housman He's difficult – tangled-up thoughts, or, anyway, tangled-up Latin –

AEH Oh – know him.

Housman – if you can believe the manuscripts – which you can't because they all come from the same one, and *that* was about as far removed from Propertius as we are from Alfred burning the cakes! He just scraped through to the invention of printing – a miracle! – the first of the Roman love elegists.

AEH Not the first, I think, strictly speaking.

Housman Oh, yes. Really and truly. Catullus was earlier but he used all sorts of metres for his Lesbia poems.

AEH Ah.

Housman Propertius's mistress was called Cynthia – 'Cynthia who first took me captive with her eyes.'

AEH *Cynthia prima suis miserum me cepit ocellis.* You mustn't forget *miserum*.

Housman Yes – *poor* me. You do know him.

AEH Oh, yes. When I was a young man at Oxford my edition of Propertius was going to replace all its forerunners and require no successor.

Housman Wouldn't that be something! I have been thinking of it, too. You see, Propertius is so corrupt (that) it seems to me, even today, *here* is a poet on which the work has not been done. All those editors!, each with his own Propertius, right up to Baehrens hot from the press! – and still (there's) the feeling that between the natural chaos of his writing and the whole hit-or-miss of the manuscripts, nobody has got the text anywhere near right. Baehrens should make everyone obsolete – isn't that why one edits Propertius? It's certainly why *I* would edit Propertius! – but one has hardly settled down with Baehrens before one is jolted out of one's chair by something like *cunctas* in one-one-five.

AEH Yes, *cunctas* for *castas* is intolerable.

Housman Well, exactly! – and he's *Baehrens*, who found the *Catullus Oxoniensis* in the Bodleian library!

AEH Baehrens is overenamoured with the manuscripts overlooked by everyone but himself. He's only human, and that's an impediment to editing a classic. To defend the credit of a scribe he'll impute any idiocy to a poet. His *conjectures*, on the other hand, are despicable trifling or barbarous depravations; yet on the whole his vanity and arrogance have deprived Baehrens of the esteem his Propertius is due.

Housman (*confused*) Oh . . . so is he good or bad?

AEH On that, you'll have to ask his mother. (*He picks up the next book.*) And here is Paley with *et* for *aut* in one-one-twenty-five. He overestimates Propertius as a poet, in my opinion, yet he has no scruple in making Propertius pray that Cynthia may love him *and also* that he may cease to love Cynthia! (*Puts the book aside.*) Some of it may be read without mirth or disgust.

Housman (*shocked*) Paley?!

AEH (*next book*) And Palmer. Palmer is a different case. He is more singularly and eminently gifted by nature than any English Latinist since Markland.

Housman (*eagerly*) Really? Palmer, then?

AEH With all his genius, in precision of thought and stability of judgement many excel him.

Housman Oh.

AEH Munro most of all.

Housman Oh, yes – Munro!

AEH And Munro you wouldn't rely on for settling a text. But Palmer has no intellectual power. Sustained thought is beyond him, so he shuns it.

Housman But I thought you said –

AEH He trusts to his felicity of instinct. When that fails him, no one can defend more stubbornly a plain corruption, or advocate more confidently an incredible conjecture, and to these defects he adds a calamitous propensity to reckless assertion.

Housman Oh! So, really, Palmer . . .

AEH (*next book*) Oh, yes. A liar and a slave. (*next book*) And him: I could teach a dog to edit Propertius like *him*. (*next book*) Oh, dear . . . well, his idea of editing a text is to change a letter or two and see what happens. If what happens can by the warmest goodwill be mistaken for sense and grammar he calls it an emendation. This is not scholarship, it is not even a sport, like hopscotch or marbles, which requires a degree of skill. It is simply a pastime, like leaning against a wall and spitting.

Housman But that's Mr Ellis! – I *went* to him for Propertius!

AEH Indeed, yes, I saw him. I thought he looked well, dangerously well. (*next book*) Ah! – Mueller! (*next book*) And Haupt! (*next book*) Rosberg! Really there's no need for you to read anything published in German in the last fifty years. Or the next fifty.

34

AEH picks up Housman's notebook casually. Housman takes it from him, a little awkwardly.

Housman Oh – that's only . . .

AEH Oh – of course. You *do* write poetry.

Housman Well, I've written poems, as one does, you know . . .

AEH One does.

Housman . . . for the poetry prize at school – quite speakable, I think –

AEH Good for you, mine were quite unspeakable.

Housman Actually, I was thinking of going in for the Newdigate – I thought the poem that won it last year was not so – how may one put it?

AEH Not such a poem as to suggest that your attempt would be a piece of impudence.

Housman But I don't know, I don't feel enough of a swell to carry off the Newdigate. Oscar Wilde of Magdalen, who went down with the Newdigate and a First in Greats, used to have tea with Ruskin. *Pater* used to have tea with *him*, in his rooms, and talk of lilies perhaps, and Michelangelo, and the French novel. The year before Wilde, it was won by a Balliol man who sent poems to Pater in the manner of the early Greek lyrics treating of matters that get you sacked at Oxford, and was duly sacked by Dr Jowett, which is rather grand behaviour in itself and almost excusable as a miscalculation of the limits of the Aesthetic. How am I to leave my mark?, a monument more lasting than bronze as Horace boasted, higher than the pyramids of kings, unyielding to wind and weather and the passage of time?

AEH Do you mean as a poet or a scholar?

Housman I don't mind.

AEH I think it helps to mind.

Housman Can't one be both?

AEH No. Not of the first rank. Poetical feelings are a peril to scholarship. There are always poetical people ready to protest that a corrrupt line is exquisite. Exquisite to whom? The Romans were foreigners writing for foreigners two millenniums ago; and for people whose gods we find quaint, whose savagery we abominate, whose private habits we don't like to talk about, but whose idea of what is exquisite is, we flatter ourselves, mysteriously identical with ours.

Housman But it *is*, isn't it? We catch our breath at the places where the breath was always caught. The poet writes to his mistress how she's killed his love – 'fallen like a flower at the field's edge where the plough touched it and passed on by'. He answers a friend's letter – 'so you won't think your letter got forgotten like a lover's apple forgotten in a good girl's lap till she jumps up for her mother and spills it to the floor blushing crimson over her sorry face'. Two thousand years in the tick of a clock – oh, forgive me, I . . .

AEH No (need), we're never too old to learn.

Housman I could weep when I think how nearly lost it was, that apple, and that flower, lying among the rubbish under a wine-vat, the last, corrupt, copy of Catullus left alive in the wreck of ancient literature. It's a cry that cannot be ignored. Do you know Munro?

AEH I corresponded with him once.

Housman I'm going to write to him. Do you think he'd send me his photograph?

AEH No. What a strange thing is a young man. You had better be a poet. Literary enthusiasm never made a scholar, and unmade many. Taste is not knowledge. A scholar's business is to add to what is known. That is all. But it is capable of giving the very greatest satisfaction, because knowledge is good. It does not have to look good or sound good or even do good. It is good just by being knowledge. And the only thing that makes it knowledge is that it is true. You can't have too much of it and there is no little too little to be worth having. There is truth and falsehood in a comma. In your text of 'The Marriage of Peleus and Thetis', Catullus says that Peleus is the protector of the power of Emathia: *Emathiae tutamen opis*, comma, *carissime nato*: how can Peleus be *carissime nato*, most dear to his son, when his son has not yet been born?

Housman I don't know.

AEH To be a scholar is to strike your finger on the page and say, 'Thou ailest here, and here.'

Housman The comma has got itself in the wrong place, hasn't it?, because there aren't any commas in the *Oxoniensis*, any more than there are capital letters – which is the other thing –

AEH Not now, nurse, let him finish.

Housman So *opis* isn't *power* with a small 'o', it's the genitive of Ops who was the mother of Jupiter. Everything comes clear when you put the comma back one place.

AEH *Emathiae tutamen*, comma, *Opis* with a capital 'O', *carissime nato*. Protector of Emathia, most dear to the son of Ops.

Housman Is that right?

AEH Oh, yes. It's right because it's true – Peleus, the protector of Emathia, *was* most dear to Jupiter the son of Ops. By taking out a comma and putting it back in a different place, sense is made out of nonsense in a poem that has been read continuously since it was first misprinted four hundred years ago. A small victory over ignorance and error. A scrap of knowledge to add to our stock. What does this remind you of? Science, of course. Textual criticism is a science whose subject is literature, as botany is the science of flowers and zoology of animals and geology of rocks. Flowers, animals and rocks being the work of nature, their sciences are exact sciences, and must answer to the authority of what can be seen and measured. Literature, however, being the work of the human mind with all its frailty and aberration, and of human fingers which make mistakes, the science of textual criticism must aim for degrees of likelihood, and the only authority it might answer to is an author who has been dead for hundreds or thousands of years. But it is a science none the less, not a sacred mystery. Reason and common sense, a congenial intimacy with the author, a comprehensive familiarity with the language, a knowledge of ancient script for those fallible fingers, concentration, integrity, mother wit and repression of self-will – these are a good start for the textual critic. In other words, almost anybody can be a botanist or a zoologist. Textual criticism is the crown and summit of scholarship. Most people, though not enough, find it dry and dull, but it is the only reason for existence for a Latin professor. I tell you this because you would not know it from the way it is conducted in the English universities. The fudge and flim-flam, the hocus-pocus and plain dishonesty that parade as scholarship in the journals would excite the professional admiration of a hawker of patent medicines. In the German universities the situation is different. Most German scholars I would put up for the Institute of Mechanics; the remainder, the Institute of Statisticians. Except for Wilamowitz who is the greatest European scholar since Richard Bentley. There are people who say that I am but they would not know it if I were. Wilamowitz, I should add, is dead. Or will be. Or will have been dead. I think it must be time for my tablet, it orders my tenses. The future perfect I have always regarded as an oxymoron. I wouldn't worry so much about your monument, if I were you. If I had my time again, I would pay more regard to those poems of Horace which tell you you will not have your time again. Life is brief and death kicks at the door impartially. Who knows how many tomorrows the gods will grant us? Now is the time, when you are young, to deck your hair with myrtle, drink the best of the wine, pluck the fruit. Seasons and moons renew themselves but neither noble name nor eloquence, no, nor righteous deeds will restore us. Night holds Hippolytus the pure of stain, Diana steads him nothing, he must stay; and Theseus leaves Pirithous in the chain the love of comrades cannot take away.

Housman What is that?

AEH A lapse.

Housman It's *'Diffugere nives'. Nec Lethaea valet Theseus abrumpere caro vincula Pirithoo.* And Theseus has not the strength to break the Lethean bonds of his beloved Pirithous.

AEH Your translation is closer.

Housman Were they comrades – Theseus and Pirithous?

AEH (Yes), companions in adventure.

Housman Companions in adventure! *There* is something to stir the soul! Was there ever a love like the love of comrades ready to lay down their lives for each other?

AEH Oh, dear.

Housman I don't mean spooniness, you know.

AEH Oh – not the love of comrades that gets you sacked at Oxford –

Housman (No! –)

AEH – not as in the lyric poets – 'when thou art kind I spend the day like a god: when thy face is turned away, it is very dark with me' –

Housman No – I mean friendship – virtue – like the Greek heroes.

AEH The Greek heroes – of course.

Housman The Argonauts . . . Achilles and Patroclus . . .

AEH Oh, yes, Achilles would get his Blue for single combat. Jason and the Argonauts would make an impression on Eights Week.

Housman Is it something to be made fun of, then?

AEH No. No.

Housman Oh, I know very well there are things not spoken of foursquare at Oxford. The passion for truth is the faintest of all human passions. In the translation of Tibullus in my College library, the *he* loved by the poet is turned into a *she*: and then when you come to the bit where this 'she' goes off with somebody's wife, the translator is equal to the crisis – he leaves it out. Horace must have been a god when he wrote '*Diffugere nives*' – the snows fled, and the seasons rolling round each year but for us, when we've had our turn, it's over! – you can't order words in English to get near it –

AEH
　　But oh, whate'er the sky-led seasons mar,
　　Moon upon moon rebuilds it with her beams:

Come *we* where Tullus and where Ancus are,
And good Aeneas, we are dust and dreams.

Housman (*cheerfully*) – yes, it's hopeless, isn't it? – one can only fall dumb, caught between your life that's gone and going! Then turn a few pages back, and Horace is in tears over some athlete, running after him in his dreams, across the Field of Mars and into the rolling waves of the Tiber! – . . . Horace!, who has lots of girls in his poems; and that's tame compared to Catullus – *he's* madly in love with Lesbia, and in between – well, the least of it is stealing kisses from – frankly – a boy who'd still be in the junior dorm at Bromsgrove.

AEH Catullus 99 – *vester* for *tuus* is the point of interest there.

Housman No, it isn't!

AEH I'm sorry.

Housman The point of interest is – what is virtue?, what is the good and the beautiful really and truly?

AEH notices the laurel on the seat. He picks it up, negligently.

AEH You think there is an answer: the lost autograph copy of life's meaning, which we might recover from the corruptions that have made it nonsense. But if there is no such copy, really and truly there is no answer. It's all in the timing. In Homer, Achilles and Patroclus were comrades, brave and pure of stain. Centuries later in a play now lost, Aeschylus brought in Eros, which I suppose we may translate as extreme spooniness; showers of kisses, and unblemished thighs. Sophocles, too; he wrote *The Loves of Achilles*: more spooniness than you'd find in a cutlery drawer, I shouldn't wonder. Also lost.

Housman How is it known, if the plays were lost?

AEH They were mentioned by critics.

Housman There were critics?

AEH Naturally – it was the cradle of democracy. Euripides wrote a *Pirithous*, the last copy having passed through the intestines of an unknown rat probably a thousand years ago if it wasn't burned by bishops – the Church's idea of the good and the beautiful excludes sexual aberration, apart from chastity, I suppose because it's the rarest. What is this? (*He holds up the laurel crown.*)

Housman It's actually mine.

AEH You'd better take it, then.

To be the fastest runner, the strongest wrestler, the best at throwing the javelin – this was virtue when Horace in his dreams ran after Ligurinus across the Field of Mars, and Ligurinus didn't lose his virtue by being caught. Virtue was practical: the athletic field was named after the god of war. If only an army should be made up of lovers and their loves! – that's not me, that's Plato, or rather Phaedrus in the Master of Balliol's nimble translation: 'although a mere handful, they would overcome the world, for each would rather die a thousand deaths than be seen by his beloved to abandon his post or throw away his arms, the veriest coward would be inspired by love'. Oh, one can sneer – the sophistry of dirty old men ogling beautiful young ones; then as now, ideals become debased. But there was such an army, a hundred and fifty pairs of lovers, the Sacred Band of Theban youths, and they were never beaten till Greek liberty died for good at the battle of Chaeronea. At the end of that day, says Plutarch, the victorious Philip of Macedon went forth to view the slain, and when he came to that place where the three hundred fought and lay dead together, he wondered, and understanding that it was the band of lovers, he shed tears and said, whoever suspects baseness in anything these men did, let him perish.

Housman I would be such a friend to someone.

AEH To dream of taking the sword in the breast, the bullet in the brain –

Housman I would.

AEH – and wake up to find the world goes wretchedly on and you will die of age and not of pain.

Housman (Well –)

AEH But lay down your life for your comrade – good lad! – lay it down like a doormat –

Housman (Oh – !)

AEH Lay it down like a card on a card-table for a kind word and a smile – lay it down like a bottle of the best to drink when your damnfool life is all but done: any more laying-downs we can think of? – oh, above all – *above all* – lay down your life like a pack on the roadside though your days of march are numbered and end with the grave. Love will not be deflected from its mischief by being called comradeship or anything else.

Housman I don't know what love is.

AEH Oh, but you do. In the Dark Ages, in Macedonia, in the last guttering light from classical antiquity, a man copied out bits from old books for his young son, whose name was Septimius; so we have one sentence from *The Loves of Achilles*. Love, said Sophocles, is like the ice held in the hand by children. A piece of ice held fast in the fist. I wish I could help you, but it's not in my gift.

Housman Love it is, then, and I will make the best of it. I'm sorry that it made you unhappy, but it's not my fault, and it can't be made good by unhappiness in another. Will you shake hands?

AEH Gladly. (*He shakes Housman's offered hand.*)

Housman What happened to Theseus and Pirithous in the end?

AEH That was the end – their last adventure was down to Hades and they were caught, bound in invisible chains. Theseus was rescued finally but he had to leave his friend behind. In the chain the love of comrades cannot take away.

Housman That's not right for *abrumpere*. If it were me I'd have put 'break away'.

AEH If it were you, you wouldn't win the Newdigate either.

Housman Oh, I don't expect I will. The subject this year is from Catullus – the lament for the Golden Age when the gods still came down to visit us, before we went to the bad.

AEH An excellent topic for a poem. False nostalgia. Ruskin said you could see the Muses dance for Apollo in Derbyshire before the railways.

Housman Where did he say that?

AEH (*points*) There.
   Is there a chamberpot under this seat?

Housman A . . .? No.

AEH Well, it probably isn't a good idea.
   We're always living in someone's golden age, it turns out: even Ruskin who takes it all so hard. A hard nut: he looks hard at everything he looks at, and everything he looks at looks hard back at him, it would drive anybody mad. In no time at all, life is like a street accident, with Ruskin raving for doctors, diverting the traffic and calling for laws to control the highway – and that's just his art criticism.

Housman I heard Ruskin lecture in my first term. Painters belayed on every side.

AEH I think we're in danger of going round again.

He stands up. Housman picks up his books. Pater and the Balliol Student enter as before.

Pater That is charmingly said. I will look at your photograph more carefully when I get home.

They leave.

AEH Yes, we are.
Pater doesn't meddle, minds his business, steps aside. When *he* looks at a thing, it melts: tone, resonance, complexity, a moment's rapture and for him alone. Life is not there to be understood, only endured and ameliorated. You'll be all right one way or the other. I was an absolutely safe First, too.

Housman Didn't you get it?

AEH No. Nor a Second, nor a Third, nor even a pass degree.

Housman You were *ploughed*?

AEH Yes.

Housman But how?

AEH That's what they all wanted to know.

Housman Oh . . .

Jackson (*off-stage*) Housman!

Pollard (*off-stage*) Housman!

Housman What happened after that?

AEH I became a clerk and lived in lodgings in Bayswater.

Pollard (*off-stage*) Hous! Picnic!

Jackson (*off-stage*) Locusts! Honey!

Housman I'm sorry, they're calling me. Did you finish your Propertius?

AEH No.

Housman Have you still got it?

AEH Oh, yes. It's in a box of papers I've arranged to be burned when I'm dead.

Jackson and Pollard arrive in the boat.

Housman (*to the boat*) I'm here.

AEH Mo . . .!

Pollard It's time to go.

Housman goes to the boat and gets in.

AEH I would have died for you but I never had the luck!

Housman Where are we going?

Pollard Hades. I've brought my Plato – will you con him with me? –

Housman I haven't looked at it. Plato is useless to explain anything except what Plato thought.

Jackson Why study him, then?

Pollard We study the ancient authors to draw lessons for our age.

Housman That's all humbug.

Pollard Is it? So it is. We study the ancient authors to get a First and a life of learned ease.

Housman We need *science* to explain the world. Jackson

46

knows more than Plato. The only reason to consider what Plato meant about anything is if it's relevant to settling the text. Which is classical scholarship, which is a science, the science of textual criticism, Jackson – we will be scientists together. I mean we will both be scientists. Pollard will be what passes as a classical scholar at Oxford, which is to be a literary critic in dead languages.

Pollard I say, did you see in the *Sketch* – Oscar Wilde's latest? 'Oh, I have worked hard all day – in the morning I put in a comma, and in the afternoon I took it out again!' Isn't that priceless?

Housman Why?

Pollard What?

Housman Oh, I see. It was a joke, you mean?

Pollard Oh – really, Housman!

> *The boat takes them away.*
> *Housman tosses the laurel wreath on the water.*

Pull on your right, Jackson.

Jackson Do you want to take the oars?

AEH *Parce, precor, precor.* Odes Four, one. Ah me, Venus, you old bawd. Where were we? Oh! – we're all here. Good. Open your Horace. Book Four, Ode One, a prayer to the Goddess of Love:

> *Intermissa, Venus, diu*
> *rursus bella moves? Parce precor, precor!*

– mercy, I pray, I pray!, or perhaps better: spare me, I beg you, I beg you! – the very words I spoke when I saw that Mr Fry was determined that *bella* is the adjective and very likely to mean beautiful, and that as eggs go with bacon it goes with Venus.

Intermissa Venus diu
rursus bella moves?

Beautiful Venus having been interrupted do you move
again?, he has Horace enquire in a rare moment of imbe-
cility, and Horace is dead as we will all be dead but while
I live I will report his cause aright. It's *war*, Mr Fry!, and
so is *bella*. Venus do you move *war*?, set in motion war,
shall we say?, or start up the war, or better: Venus are you
calling me to arms, *rursus*, again, *diu*, after a long time,
intermissa, having been interrupted, or suspended if you
like, and what is it that has been suspended? Two centuries ago Bentley read *intermissa* with *bella*, *war* having
been suspended, not Venus, Mr Fry, and – yes – Mr
Carsen – and also Miss Frobisher, good morning, you'll
forgive us for starting without you – and now all is clear,
is it not? Ten years after announcing in Book Three that
he was giving up love, the poet feels desire stirring once
more and begs for mercy: 'Venus, are you calling me to
arms again after this long time of truce? Spare me, I beg
you, I beg you!' Miss Frobisher smiles, with little cause
that I know of. If Jesus of Nazareth had had before him
the example of Miss Frobisher getting through the Latin
degree papers of the London University Examinations
Board he wouldn't have had to fall back on camels and
the eyes of needles, and Miss Frobisher's name would be a
delightful surprise to encounter in Matthew, Chapter 19;
as would, even more surprisingly, the London University
Examinations Board. Your name is not Miss Frobisher?
What is your name? Miss Burton. I'm very sorry. I stand
corrected. If Jesus of Nazareth had had before him the
example of Miss Burton getting through the . . . Oh, dear,
I hope it is not I who have made you cry. You don't mind?
You don't mind when I make you cry? Oh, Miss Burton,
you must try to mind a little. Life is in the minding. Here
is Horace at the age of fifty pretending not to mind, verse

29, *me nec femina nec puer, iam nec spes animi credula mutui* – where's the verb? anyone? *iuvat*, thank you, it delights me not, what doesn't? – neither woman nor boy, nor the *spes credula*, the credulous hope, *animi mutui* – the trusting hope of love returned, *nec*, nor, that's four *nec*s and a fifth to come before the 'but', that's why we call it poetry – *nec certare iuvat mero* – yes, to compete in wine, that'll do for the moment, and *nec* – what? – *nec vincire novis tempora floribus*, rendered by Mr Howard as to tie new flowers to my head, Tennyson would hang himself – never mind, here is Horace not minding: I take no pleasure in woman or boy, nor the trusting hope of love returned, nor matching drink for drink, nor binding fresh-cut flowers around my brow – *but* – *sed* – *cur heu, Ligurine, cur* –

Jackson is seen as a runner running towards us from the dark, getting no closer.

– but why, Ligurinus, alas why this unaccustomed tear trickling down my cheek? – why does my glib tongue stumble to silence as I speak? At night I hold you fast in my dreams, I run after you across the Field of Mars, I follow you into the tumbling waters, and you show no pity.

Blackout.

Act Two

The summit of 'Mount Pisgah' at sunset, Housman, aged twenty-two, and Katharine Housman, aged nineteen, looking out to the west. Some breeze.

Housman ... All the land of Gilead, unto Dan, and all Naphtali, and the land of Ephraim, and Manasseh, and all the land of Judah unto the utmost sea, but not including Wales which I give to the Methodists.

Kate But what happened, Alfred?

Housman That's what they all wanted to know.

Kate It's the end of fun. We're all frightened of you now, except me, and I am, too. Father feels the blow, in the rain of blows. We're a house of scrimping and tip-toeing and only one fire allowed in winter. Clemence does the books to a halfpenny. Mr Millington always said if she'd been a boy he'd have been glad to have her in his Sixth Form.

Housman Millington thought the worst thing that could happen to me was that I'd get a Second. Well, he was wrong about that. He's asked me to take the Sixth for classics from time to time, an act of charity. I'll be teaching young Basil.

Kate I wish I'd had you to teach me, I wouldn't be the dunce. You put us all on the lawn once to be the sun and planets. I was the earth, and did pirouettes round Laurence while you skipped around me for my moonlight. That's all the astronomy I ever knew. Will you be a schoolmaster, then?

Housman Only while I'm waiting to take the Civil Service exam.

Kate The Civil Service?

Housman A Servant of the Crown.

Kate Like a diplomat?

Housman Yes, exactly. Or a postman. My friend Jackson has got himself into Her Majesty's Patent Office. That would be convenient for the Reading Room of the British Museum. I'm going to carry on with classics. Look at Clee now – how blue it gets when the sun goes down!

Kate Oh, yes! – our Promised Land!

Housman I stopped believing in God, by the way.

Kate Oh, that's just Oxford.

Housman I was waiting by the river for my friends Jackson and Pollard. You don't know Jackson. Pollard is the one who came to stay once. Mamma disapproved of his letting her see him approach the door of the lavatory. He lacked the proper furtiveness . . . Well, I was waiting for them on a bench by the river and it came upon me that I was alone, and there was no help for anything.

Kate Mamma would die if she could hear you.

Housman I won't mention it at family prayers.

Kate Oxford has made you smart. Do you remember what our real mother was like?

Housman Oh, yes: when she was ill I sat with her all the time. We used to pray together for her to get better, and she talked to me as if I were grown up.

Kate *She* can hear you.

Housman I stopped believing in *that* part when I was thirteen.

Kate That was only to punish Him for mother dying.

Housman And by God, He stayed punished.

Darkness.
  In a spotlight, 'Bunthorne' in Patience *by Gilbert and Sullivan, is singing.*

Bunthorne (*sings*)
'Though the Philistines may jostle,
you may rank as an apostle
in the high aesthetic band,
if you walk down Piccadilly
with a poppy or a lily
in your medieval hand . . .'

Bunthorne exits.
  A station platform at night, the 'Underground–Overground' Steam Railway.
  Housman, aged twenty-three, and Jackson, aged twenty-four, dressed as for 'the office', are waiting for the train. Housman has a Journal of Philology, *Jackson an evening paper.*

Jackson Wasn't it magnificent? A landmark, Hous!

Housman I thought it was . . . quite jolly . . .

Jackson Quite jolly? It was a watershed! D'Oyly Carte has made the theatre *modern*.

Housman (*surprised*) You mean Gilbert and Sullivan?

Jackson What? No. No, the *theatre*.

Housman (Oh, I see.)

Jackson The first theatre lit entirely by electricity!

Housman Dear old Mo . . .

Jackson D'Oyly Carte's new Savoy is a triumph.

Housman . . . you're the only London theatre critic worthy of the name. 'The new electrified Savoy is a triumph. The contemptible flickering gas-lit St James's –'

Jackson (*overlapping*) Oh, I know you're ragging me . . .

Housman '. . . the murky malodorous Haymarket . . . the unscientific Adelphi . . .'

Jackson But it was exciting, wasn't it, Hous? Every age thinks it's the modern age, but this one really is. Electricity is going to change everything. Everything! We had an electric corset sent in today.

Housman One that lights up?

Jackson I've never thought of it before, but in a way the Patent Office is the gatekeeper to the new age.

Housman An Examiner of Electrical Specifications may be, but it's not the same with us toiling down in Trade Marks. I had sore throat lozenges today, an application to register a wonderfully woebegone giraffe – raised rather a subtle point in Trade Marks regulation, actually: it seems there is already a giraffe at large, wearing twelve styles of celluloid collar, but, and here's the nub, a *happy* giraffe, in fact a preening self-satisfied giraffe. The question arises – is the registered giraffe Platonic?, are all God's giraffes *in esse et in posse* to be rendered unto the Houndsditch Novelty Collar Company?

Jackson It's true, then – a classical education fits a fellow for anything.

Housman Well, I consulted my colleague Chamberlain – he's compiling the new Index – I don't think he's altogether sound, Chamberlain, he put John the Baptist under Mythological Characters –

Jackson Do you know what someone said?

Housman – and a monk holding a tankard under Biblical Subjects.

Jackson Will you tell me what happened?

Housman Oh, we found for the lozenges.

Jackson Someone said you ploughed yourself on purpose.

Housman Pollard?

Jackson No. But they had him in to ask about you.

Housman I saw Pollard in the Reading Room.

Jackson What did *he* have to say?

Housman Nothing. It was the Reading Room. We adjusted our expressions briefly.

Jackson We got what we wanted, Pollard at the British Museum and here's me with an Examinership and three hundred a year with prospects . . . You were cleverer than any of us, Hous!

Housman I didn't get what I wanted, that's true, but I want what I've got.

Jackson Pushing a pen at thirty-eight shillings a week.

Housman But here we are, you and I, we eat the same meals in the same digs, catch the same train to work in the same office, and the work is easy, I've got time to do classics . . . and friendship is all, sometimes I'm so happy, it makes me dizzy – and, look, I have prospects, too!, I'm published! (*He shows Jackson the journal.*) I was saving it for cocoa.

Jackson I say! –

Housman The *Journal of Philology*. See?

Jackson 'Horatiana' . . . 'A. E. Housman' – I say! . . . What is it?

Housman It's putting people right about what Horace really wrote.

Jackson Horace!

Housman Only bits. I'm working on Propertius really.

Jackson Well done, Hous! We must celebrate!

Housman But we have – that's why I . . .

Jackson (*reminded*) Oh, but I still owe you for . . .

Housman No, it was my idea, and anyway you thought the electricians were the best thing in it.

Jackson The girls were pretty, and the tunes, it was only the story.

Housman The whole thing was silly.

Jackson *Jolly*, you said. You don't have to agree with me all the time.

Housman I don't!

Jackson Well, you do, you know, Hous – you should stick to your own opinions more.

Housman Well, that's a bit thick when I've just told Richard Bentley (that) his 'securesque' in three twenty-six won't do!

Jackson Who? – Oh, *veni, vidi, vici* . . .
What gets *my* goat, actually, if you want to know, is that the fellow isn't worth the fuss, none of them are – I mean, what *use* is he to anyone?

Housman *Use*? . . . I know it's not useful like electricity, but it's exciting, really and truly, to spot something –

Jackson What?

Housman – to be the first person for thousands of years to read the verse as it was written – What?

Jackson I mean these Aesthetes – the show . . .

Housman (Oh – !)

Jackson What gets *me* is all this attention – you can't open a newspaper (without . . .), and cartoons in *Punch* every time he opens his mouth being aesthetic and better than ordinary people working at proper things . . . I mean what's he ever *done?*, and now an operetta, for heaven's sake, to make him the talk of the town twice over – *what has he ever done?*, that's what I'd like to know.

Housman Well, I . . . He's had a book of poems . . .

Jackson I've got nothing against poetry, don't think I have, I like a good poem as well as the next man, but you don't find Tennyson flouncing about Piccadilly and trying to be witty, do you? – and all that posing and dressing up, it's not manly, if you ask me, Hous.

Housman It wasn't him with the electric corset, was it?

Jackson There were several at Oxford, I remember.

Housman Do you remember he said your leg was a poem?

Jackson Which one?

Housman Left. Oh – Wilde. Oscar Wilde.

Jackson Oscar Wilde was at Oxford with *us?*

Housman In our first year, he went down with a First in Greats. I went to Warren, his tutor at Magdalen. You don't remember?

Jackson There was a Wyld who bowled a bit, left arm round the wicket . . .

Housman No, no . . . Blue china . . .

Jackson Wait a minute. Velvet knickerbockers! Well, I'm damned! I knew he wasn't the full shilling!

> *Noise and lights: arriving train. Darkness.*
> *A room – the billiard room, perhaps – in a London club, 1885, at night.*
> *Labouchere and Harris, in full evening dress – perhaps – with brandy and cigars – for example – are playing billiards, or not.*
> *A third man, Stead, wears an almost shabby office suit. He has a full beard and the fanatical gleam of a prophet. He is scanning a newspaper in a professional manner.*

Labouchere We invented Oscar, we bodied him forth. Then we floated him. Then we kited the stock. When D'Oyly Carte took *Patience* to New York, he had the idea of bringing Oscar to America and exhibiting him as the original aesthetic article for purposes of publicity, and Oscar did him proud before he was off the boat – 'Mr Wilde Disappointed by Atlantic' – remember that, Stead?, you gave it space in the *Gazette*, and I printed the Atlantic's reply in *Truth* – 'Atlantic Disappointed by Mr Wilde'. I wrote him up nicely, and Oscar, who didn't know it was all a ramp, told people over there, 'Henry Labouchere is one of my heroes' . . . all in all, most satisfactory, a job well done. But now he's got away from us. No matter where we cut the string, the kite won't fall. The ramp is over and the stock keeps rising. When he came home and had the cheek to lecture in Piccadilly on his impressions of America, I filled three columns under the heading 'Exit Oscar'. I dismissed him, no doubt to his surprise, as an effeminate phrase-maker. I counted up the number of times he used the word 'beautiful', 'lovely' or 'charming', and it came to eighty-six. You'd think that would sink anybody, but not at all . . . He went off round the provinces and people paid good money to be told they were provincial . . . their houses were ugly inside and out, their dress dowdy, their husbands dull, their wives plain, and their opinions on art worthless. Meanwhile, Oscar himself has never done anything.

Harris You were on the wrong end of the string, Labby.

Labouchere Up, up, up . . . It shakes one's faith in the operation of a moral universe by journalism.

Stead It's the aimless arrow that brings us down, the arrow fledged with one of our own feathers.

Harris You really ought to edit the Old Testament, old man.

Labouchere He does.

Stead The *Pall Mall Gazette* is testament enough that the Lord is at my elbow, and was there today when I – yes, I! – forced Parliament to pass the Criminal Law Amendment Act.

Harris You know, Stead, most people think you're mad. They thought so even before you bought a thirteen-year-old virgin for £5 to prove a point. A wonderful stunt, I wouldn't deny – I doff my hat. When I took over the *Evening News* I edited the paper with the best in me at twenty-eight. The circulation wouldn't budge. So, I edited the paper as a boy of fourteen. The circulation started to rise and never looked back.

Stead No, by heavens, Harris! In the right hands the editor's pen is the sceptre of power! For us, life can once more be brilliant as in the heroic days. In my first campaign, when I was still a young man in the provinces, I roused the north against Lord Beaconsfield's Russian Policy and the Turkish atrocities in Bulgaria. 'The honour of the Bulgarian virgins,' I told my readers, 'is in the hands of the electors of Darlington.' I heard the clear call of the voice of God in 1876: I heard it again last year when I forced the government to send General Gordon to Khartoum; and I heard it in my campaign which today has given thirteen-, fourteen-, and fifteen-year-old British virgins the protection of Parliament.

Harris General Gordon got his head cut off.

Stead Whether he did or not –

Harris He did.

Stead – we journalists have a divine mission to be the tribunes of the people.

Harris The Turko-Russia war was my blooding as a journalist. I was with General Skobeleff at the battle of Plevna.

Labouchere (*to Stead*) I'm a Member of Parliament, I don't have to be a journalist to be a tribune of the people.
  (*to Harris*) No, you weren't, Frank. You were at Brighton.
  (*to Stead*) The Criminal Law Amendment Act is badly drawn up and will do more harm than good, as I said in my paper.
  (*to Harris*) In '76 you were a French tutor at Brighton College, or so you told Hattie during the interval at *Phedre*.

Harris That was a flight of fancy.

Labouchere (*to Stead*) The Bill should have been referred to a Select Committee, and would have been but for the government being stampeded by your disgusting articles.

Harris Traditionally, Parliament has always been the protector of the British virgin, but usually on a first come first served basis.

Labouchere You have made the *Pall Mall Gazette* look sensational even when there's nothing sensational in it, but the Maiden Tribute campaign was a disgrace to decency – you had errand boys reading about filthy goings-on which concerned nobody but their sisters.

Harris Is it true you caught a mouse in the *Gazette* office and ate it on toast?

Stead Perfectly true.
   (*to Labouchere*) When I came down from Darlington to join the *Gazette* –

Harris Up.

Stead – it never sold more than 13,000 copies and never deserved to – it kept the reader out.

Harris Up from Darlington.

Stead I introduced the crosshead in '81, the illustration in '82, the interview in '83, the personal note, the signed article –

Labouchere Why did you eat a mouse?

Stead I wanted to know what it tasted like.

Labouchere You should have asked me. I ate them in Paris during the Siege, and rats and cats.

Stead I invented the New Journalism!

Labouchere We didn't eat the rats till we'd eaten all the cats.

Stead I gave virtue a voice Parliament couldn't ignore.

Labouchere Then we ate the dogs. When there were no

dogs left we ate the animals in the zoo.

Stead Item! The age of consent raised from thirteen to sixteen.

Labouchere I sent my despatches out by balloon and made my name. I suppose you were in the Siege of Paris, too, Frank.

Harris No, in 1870 I was building the Brooklyn Bridge.

Stead Item! Girls in moral danger may be removed from their parents by the courts.

Labouchere *That'll* be a dead letter.

Stead But it was your Amendment.

Labouchere Anybody with any sense on the backbenches was pitch-forking Amendments in to get the government to admit it had a pig's breakfast on its hands and withdraw it. I forced a division on raising the age of consent to twenty-one!, and two people voted for it. My final effort was the Amendment on indecency between male persons, and God help me, it went through on the nod – (it had) nothing to do with the Bill we were supposed to be debating; normally it would have been ruled out of order, but everyone wanted to be shot of the business, prorogue Parliament, and get on to the General Election.

Stead But – but surely – you *intended* the Bill to address a contemporary evil –?

Labouchere Nothing of the sort. I intended to make the Bill absurd to any sensible person left in what by then was a pretty thin House . . . but that one got away, so now a French kiss and what-you-fancy between two chaps safe at home with the door shut is good for two years with or without hard labour. It's a funny old world.

Stead Then your mischief was timely. London shows all

the indications of falling into the abyss of perverse eroticism that encompassed the fall of Greece and Rome.

Labouchere What indications are they?

Stead There is a scepticism of what is morally elevating, a taste for the voluptuous and the forbidden in French literature. Our Aesthetes look to Paris for their sins, which I will not name, which are so odious they should never have been allowed to leave France.

Harris Actually, in Greece and Rome sodomy was rarely associated with a taste for French novels, it was the culture of the athletic ground and the battlefield; as in Sparta, for example, or the Sacred Band of Thebes. It so happens that I was wandering through Greece in October of 1880, travelling sometimes on foot, sometimes on horse, putting up at monasteries or with shepherds in their huts, and I arrived finally at Thebes. There was a German archaeologist there who said his name was Schliemann –

Labouchere Harris, do you *ever* tell the truth?

Harris – who told us that a young Greek lad had just discovered a very large grave at Chaeronea near by, right under the stone lion erected by Philip of Macedon to commemorate his victory there in 338 BC. It was at the battle of Chaeronea, you remember, where, according to Plutarch, a hundred and fifty pairs of lovers pledged to defend Thebes from the invader fought and died to the last man. Well, I stayed on there until we had uncovered 297 skeletons, buried together.

Labouchere So it was you!

Harris They were in two layers, packed like sardines. You could still see where the Macedonian lances smashed arms, ribs, skulls . . . Most extraordinary thing I've ever seen.

Open ground. Summer afternoon, 1885.

Housman, aged twenty-six, is comfortable on the grass, reading the Journal of Philology. *Chamberlain, a contemporary, is sitting up, reading the* Daily Telegraph *or similar. They are inattentive spectators at a suburban athletics meeting, the sounds of which are now some feeble applause, a few random shouts, perhaps a band-stand; all of these at a distance. A bag containing bot-tled beer and sandwiches lies by them.*

Chamberlain What do you think, Housman? Five pounds for a virgin. Would that mean one go? . . .

Housman You can't have two goes at the same virgin.

Chamberlain . . . or do you get her to keep?, I mean. What *are* the parliamentary reports coming to?

Housman Is that the quarter-mile lining up? I can't see Jackson.

Chamberlain It probably isn't, then.

Housman (*anxious*) Are you sure? We haven't come all the way out to Ealing to miss it.

Chamberlain 'Mr Labouchere, Lib., Northampton . . .' . . . *he* has a way with him.

Housman Or is that the half?

Chamberlain There's no way of telling at the start, it all depends on where they stop. 'Mr Labouchere's Amendment . . .' Oh dear oh dear oh dear, well, that's opened up the north-west passage for every blackmailer in town; you'd think they'd know, wouldn't you? Educated at Eton and Trinity, too, so what's he got left to be shocked about?

Housman I do believe it is the quarter-mile, you know. (*He stands up as a distant starting pistol is heard.*) Can you see him?

Chamberlain finally looks up from his paper.

Chamberlain The quarter-mile is a flat race, isn't it? – that's hurdles. (*He returns to his paper.*)

Housman (*relieved*) Oh, yes . . . it's after the 220 hurdles.

Chamberlain Running late.

Housman (No, 220 yards . . .)

Chamberlain Sit down, you're like a nervous girl.

> *Distant shouts, some applause. Chamberlain studies his newspaper.*

No offence, old chap. I like you more than anyone I know. I even like you for the way you stick to Jackson. But he'll never want what you want. You'll have to find it somewhere else or you'll be unhappy, even unhappier. I know whereof I speak. I don't mind you knowing. I know you won't tell on me at the office. You're the straightest, kindest man I know and I'm sorry for you, that's all. I'm sorry if I spoke out of turn.

> *A distant starting pistol. Chamberlain stands up. They watch the progress of the runners, for form's sake, silent, separate, remote from the fact. The race takes nearly a minute: the pauses and speeches are in real time.*
> *Long pause.*

He'll be in the first three if he keeps it up.

> *Long pause.*

Housman (*watching the runners*) What do I want?

Chamberlain Nothing which you'd call indecent, though I don't see what's wrong with it myself. You want to be brothers-in-arms, to have him to yourself . . . to be ship-wrecked together, (to) perform valiant deeds to earn his

admiration, to save him from certain death, to die for him – to die in his arms, like a Spartan, kissed once on the lips . . . or just run his errands in the meanwhile. You want him to know what cannot be spoken, and to make the perfect reply, in the same language. (*Pause. Still without inflection*) He's going to win it. (*Finally he warms into excitement as the race passes in front of them.*) By God, he is! Come on, Jackson! Up the Patent Office! . . .
. . . He's won it!

Chamberlain slaps Housman on the back in unaffected joy. Housman thaws, catching up.

Housman He won!

Chamberlain We should have brought champagne!

Housman No, he likes his bottle of Biblical Subject. (*embarrassed*) Well . . .

Chamberlain Come on, then – I'm thirsty with all that running.

Pollard, aged twenty-six, arrives hot and bothered, in office dress, carrying a Pink 'Un *edition of the Saturday afternoon newspaper.*

Pollard Housman! – there you are! Was that the quarter?

Housman Pollard – you duffer! You've missed it! He won!

Pollard Damn! I mean – you know what I mean. I couldn't get here a minute sooner. I bet I ran faster from the station than Jackson.
(*to Chamberlain*) How do you do?

Housman Chamberlain, this is Pollard; Pollard, this is Chamberlain.

Chamberlain Very pleased to meet you.

Housman He's at the British Museum.

Pollard (*to Chamberlain*) Not an exhibit, I work at the library.

Housman You are an exhibit . . . (*He tidies Pollard's collar and tie.*) Here, look. There. We've got a picnic.

Pollard Ah, locusts and honey.

Housman The three of us used to take a boat down to Hades, with a picnic – where's Mo?

Pollard It was only once.

Housman We were chums together at St John's –

Chamberlain (Hades . . .?)

Housman – oh! – Chamberlain is an expert on the Baptist, that well-known mythological character.

Pollard Really?

Chamberlain He was a water-biscuit. Yes, it's confusing but we keep an open mind at the Trade Marks Registry.

Housman Here he is – *victor ludorum*.

Jackson joins them.

Pollard *Ave, Ligurine!*

Housman Jolly well done, Mo!

Chamberlain I say! What was your time?

Jackson Oh, I don't know, it's only a race, don't make a fuss. Fifty-four, apparently. Hello, Pollard. (*accepting a bottle of beer from Housman*) Thanks. This is sporting of you. And sandwiches!

Chamberlain (*offering sandwiches*) Age before beauty.

Jackson (*declining*) I'll get changed first. (*to Pollard*) Got the *Pink 'Un*? Good man. (*taking it*) How were the Australians doing?

Pollard At what?

Jackson Oh, *really*, Pollard! (*He laughs, leaving with his beer and the* Pink 'Un.)

Pollard The paper is full of white-slave traffic today. Apparently we lead the world in exporting young women to Belgium.

Chamberlain It's disgusting, the way the papers have been hashing it up.

Pollard Hushing it up?

Chamberlain Not *hushing* it up. *Hashing* it up.

Pollard Oh . . .

Pollard and Housman catch each other's eye and laugh at the same thought.

Chamberlain (*after a pause*) Well, we'll never know.

Housman It's nothing much to know anyway. Before books were printed, often you'd have one person dictating to two or three copyists . . .

Pollard . . . then, hundreds of years later, there'd be a manuscript in one place that's got 'hushing it up' and one in another place that's got 'hashing it up', only in Latin, of course, and people like Housman here arguing about which the author really wrote. Have you got something in there (the *Journal*)?

Chamberlain Why?

Housman (No.)

Pollard And, of course, the copies get copied, so then you can argue about which copies come first and which scribes had bad habits – oh, the fun is endless.

Chamberlain But there's no way to tell if they both make sense.

Housman One of them always makes the better sense if you can get into the writer's mind, without prejudices.

Pollard And then you publish your article insisting it was really 'lashing it up'.

Chamberlain Why?

Pollard Why? So that other people can write articles insisting it was 'mashing it up' or 'washing it up'.

Chamberlain Toss a coin – I would.

Pollard That's another good method. (I'm) only teasing, Housman, don't look so down in the mouth.

Chamberlain (*gets up*) I'm off, apologize for me to Jackson. I've got to meet someone in the West End at five.

Pollard There's still plenty of trains.

Chamberlain I came on my bicycle.

Pollard Goodness!

Chamberlain It was very nice to meet you.

Pollard Likewise. Yes, don't keep the lady waiting!

Chamberlain Oh, you've guessed my secret. Thanks, Housman. I'll see you on Monday.

Housman I'm sorry you have to go. Thank you.

Chamberlain Wouldn't have missed it.

Pollard Nor I.

Chamberlain But you did.

Pollard Oh, that.

Chamberlain goes.

Housman No need to tell Jackson – he'd be disappointed. Why did you call him Ligurinus?

Pollard Wasn't it Ligurinus? – running over the Campus Martius? (*From his pocket he takes about twenty handwritten pages.*) Thanks for this.

Housman What did you think?

Pollard You won't expect me to judge it. I'm no Propertius scholar.

Housman But you've read him.

Pollard I read a few of the elegies in my third year but Propertius is too rough-cornered for my taste.

Housman Yes – mine, too.

Pollard (But –?!)

Housman To be a scholar, the first thing you have to learn is that scholarship is nothing to do with taste; speaking, of course, as a Higher Division Clerk in Her Majesty's Patent Office. Propertius looked to me like a garden gone to wilderness, and not a very interesting garden either, but what an opportunity! – it was begging to be put back in order. Better still, various nincompoops thought they had already done it . . . hacking about, to make room for their dandelions. So far, I've improved the vulgate in about two hundred places.

Pollard laughs.

But I have.

Pollard I'm sure you have.

Housman What worries you about it?

Pollard Well, the tone of some of it, it's a bit breathtaking. It's all right me reading it, because I know what a soft old thing you are underneath, but it isn't the way scholars generally deal with each other, is it?

Housman (*lightly*) Oh, Bentley and Scaliger were far ruder.

Pollard But that was centuries ago, and you're not Bentley, not yet anyway. Who is Postgate?

Housman Oh, he's a good man, one of the best of the younger Propertius critics –

Pollard (What –?!) (*He finds his place, on the last page.*)

Housman – he's a professor at UCL.

Pollard (*reading*) '. . . makes nonsense of the whole elegy from beginning to end . . .'

Housman Well, he does. '*Voces*' in verse 33 is an emendation to frighten children in their beds.

Pollard ' . . . But I imagine these considerations will have occurred to Mr Postgate himself ere now, or will have been pointed out to him by his friends.' . . . It's so disrespectful.

Housman Your point being that I'm a clerk in the Patent Office.

Pollard (*hotly*) No! – I'm *not* saying that!

Housman I'm sorry. Let's not fall out. Have another Biblical Subject.

They open two bottles of beer.

Pollard (*explaining*) I was only thinking suppose one day you put in for a lectureship at University College and your Mr Postgate was on the selection committee.

Housman I'd only apply for a Chair at UCL.

Pollard (*laughs*) Oh . . . Housman, what will become of you?

Housman You're my only friend who might understand, don't let me down. If I'm disrespectful it's because it's important and not a game anyone can play. I could have given Chamberlain a proper answer. Scholarship doesn't need to wriggle out of it with a joke. It's where we're nearest to our humanness. Useless knowledge for its own sake. Useful knowledge is good, too, but it's for the faint-hearted, an elaboration of the real thing, which is only to shine some light, it doesn't matter where on what, it's the light itself, against the darkness, it's what's left of God's purpose when you take away God. It doesn't mean I don't care about the poetry. I do. *Diffugere nives* goes through me like a spear. Nobody makes it stick like Horace that you're a long time dead – dust and shadow, and no good deeds, no eloquence, will bring you back. I think it's the most beautiful poem in Latin or Greek there ever was; but in verse 15 Horace never wrote '*dives*' which is in all the texts, and I'm pretty sure I know what he did write. Anyone who says 'So what?' got left behind five hundred years ago when we became modern, that's why it's called Humanism. The recovery of ancient texts is the highest task of all – Erasmus, bless him. It is work to be done. Posterity has a brisk way with manuscripts: scholarship is a small redress against the vast unreason of what is taken from us – it's not just the worthless that perish, Jesus doesn't save.

Pollard Stop – stop it, Housman! – the sun is shining, it's Saturday afternoon! – I'm happy! The best survives because it is the best.

Housman Oh . . . Pollard. Have you ever seen a cornfield after the reaping? Laid flat to stubble, and here and there, unaccountably, miraculously spared, a few stalks still upright. Why those? There is no reason. Ovid's Medea, the Thyestes of Varius who was Virgil's friend and considered by some his equal, the lost Aeschylus trilogy of the Trojan war . . . gathered to oblivion in *sheaves*, along with hundreds of Greek and Roman authors known only for fragments or their names alone – and here and there a cornstalk, a thistle, a poppy, still standing, but as to purpose, signifying nothing.

Pollard I know what you want.

Housman What do I want?

Pollard A monument. Housman was here.

Housman Oh, you've guessed my secret.

Pollard A mud pie against the incoming tide.

Housman (Oh, that's) a fine way to speak of my edition of Propertius.

Pollard (*toasting*) To you and your Propertius. Who's that with Jackson?, do you know her?

Housman No. Yes. She came to the office.

Pollard Well, don't stare.

Housman I'm not.

Pollard (*toasting*) Coupled with the British Museum library! The aggregate of human progress made stackable!

Housman (*toasting*) Making a stand against the natural and merciful extinction of the unreadable! How very British of it. Bring back the manuscript . . .

Pollard Is it over?, people seem to be leaving.

Housman starts packing up the picnic.

Housman When you consider the ocean of bilge brought forth by the invention of printing, it does make you wonder about this boon of civilization. I wonder about it every time I open the *Journal of Philology*.

No. They're gathering . . . Oh! – they're giving out the trophies! Come on!

They go. Housman taking the picnic bag.

Elsewhere – night.
Jackson, in his pyjamas and dressing-gown, reads aloud from a handwritten page; a modest silver trophy-cup perhaps in evidence.

Jackson
'Blest as one of the gods is he,
The Youth who fondly sits by thee,
And hears and sees thee all the while
Softly speak and sweetly smile.
For while I gaze with trembling heart . . .'

Mmm. Did you write this?

Housman comes with two mugs of cocoa. He is wearing day-clothes.

Housman Well, Sappho, really, more or less.

Jackson (*ponders*) Mmm. What's that one you used to have about kisses?

Housman Catullus. 'Give me a thousand kisses and then a hundred more.'

Jackson Yes. She might think that's a bit hot, though. It should really be about me being unhappy and ticking her off for her unfaithfulness, and at the same time willing to forgive. Where's the one again where I'm carving her name on trees?

Housman Propertius. But honestly, that's a bit raving – she's only said she's staying in to wash her hair.

Jackson But I'd got tickets and everything! After being at her beck and call . . .

Housman *Quinque tibi potui servire (fidelitur annos)*.

Jackson What?

Housman Five years your faithful slave.

Jackson Exactly. Two weeks anyway.

Housman The problem we're up against here is that the ticking-off ones make her out to be a harlot, and the happy ones make her out to be, well, *your* harlot . . . so I think the way to go is more *carpe diem*, gather ye rose-buds while you may, the grave's a fine and private place but none I think do there embrace.

Jackson She'd never believe I wrote that.

Housman Dear old Mo, what will become of you?

Jackson Orchestra stalls, too.

Housman Oh, *well*! – 'If that's the price for kisses due, it's the last kiss I steal from *you*' – written to a boy, but never mind – interesting poem, by the way: *vester* for *tuus* –

Jackson She thinks you're sweet on me.

Housman – plural for singular, the first use. What?

Jackson Rosa said you're sweet on me.

Housman What did she mean?

Jackson Well, you know.

Housman What did you say?

Jackson I said it was nonsense. We're chums. We've been

chums since Oxford, you, me and Pollard.

Housman Did she think Pollard was sweet on you?

Jackson She didn't talk about Pollard. You're not, are you, Hous?

Housman You're my best friend.

Jackson That's what I said, like . . .

Housman Theseus and Pirithous.

Jackson The Three Musketeers.

Housman What did she say?

Jackson She hasn't read it.

Housman I don't understand. You mean, just from Saturday, just from going home together on the train from Ealing?

Jackson I suppose so. Yes. It was odd Chamberlain being there that day.

Housman Why?

Jackson Well, it was just odd. An odd coincidence. I was going to mention it.

Housman Mention what?

Jackson Mention that perhaps you shouldn't get to be pals with him too much, it may be misunderstood.

Housman You think Chamberlain is sweet on me?

Jackson No, of course not. But one has heard things about Chamberlain at the office. I'm sorry now I mentioned him! I know I'm all hobnails but you're all right about it, aren't you, Hous? You see, I'm awfully strong on Rosa, she's not like other girls, she's not what I'd call a *girl* at all, you saw that for yourself, she's a woman, we love each other.

Housman I'm glad for you, Mo. I liked her very much.

Jackson (*pleased*) Did you? I knew you would. You're a good pal to me and I hope I am to you. I knew I only had to ask you and that would be the end of it. I'll tell her she's a cuckoo. Shake hands?

Jackson puts out his hand, Housman takes it.

Housman Gladly.

Jackson Still pals.

Housman Comrades.

Jackson Like whoever they were.

Housman Theseus and Pirithous. They were kings. They met on the field of battle to fight to the death, but when they saw each other, each was struck in admiration for his adversary, so they became comrades instead and had many adventures together. Theseus was never so happy as when he was with his friend. They weren't sweet on each other. They loved each other, as men loved each other in the heroic age, in virtue, paired together in legend and poetry as the pattern of comradeship, the chivalric ideal of virtue in the ancient world. Virtue! What happened to it? It had a good run – centuries! – it was still virtue in Socrates to admire a beautiful youth, virtue to be beautiful and admired, it was still there, grubbier and a shadow of itself but still there, for my Roman poets who competed for women and boys as fancy took them; virtue in Horace to shed tears of love over Ligurinus on the athletic field. Well, not any more, eh, Mo? Virtue is what women have to lose, the rest is vice. Pollard thinks I'm sweet on you, too, though he hardly knows he thinks it. Will you mind if I go to live somewhere but close by?

Jackson Why?
  Oh . . .

Housman We'll still be friends, won't we?

Jackson Oh!

Housman Of *course* Rosa knew! – of *course* she'd know!

Jackson Oh!

Housman Did you really not know even for a minute?

Jackson How could I know? You seem just like . . . you know, normal. You're not one of those Aesthete types or anything – (*angrily*) how could I know?!

Housman You mean if I dressed like the Three Musketeers you'd have suspected?
You're half my life.
We took a picnic down to Hades. There was a dog on the island there, a friendly lost dog and not even wet, a mystery, he jumped into the boat to be rescued. Do you remember the dog? Pollard and I were arguing about English or Latin being best for poetry – the dog was subjoined: lost dog loves young man – dog young lost man loves, loves lost young man dog, you can't beat Latin: shuffle the words to suit, the endings tell you which loves what, who's young, who lost, if you can't read Latin go home, you've missed it! You kissed the dog. After that day, everything else seemed futile and ridiculous: the ridiculous idea that one's life was poised on the reading course . . .

Jackson (*puzzled*) Dog?

Housman (*cries out*) Oh, if only you hadn't said anything! We could have carried on the same!

Jackson (*an announcement*) It's not your fault. That's what I say. It's terrible but it's not your fault. You won't find me casting the first stone. (*Pause.*) We'll be just like before.

Housman Do you mean it, Mo?

Jackson No one will know it from me. We've been pals a long time.

Housman Thank you.

Jackson It's rotten luck but it'll be our secret. You'll easily find some decent digs round here – we'll catch the same train to work as always, and I bet before you know it you'll meet the right girl and we'll all three be chuckling over this – Rosa, I mean. What about that? I dare say I've surprised you! All right? Shake on it?

Jackson puts out his hand.
Darkness, except on Housman.

Housman
He would not stay for me; and who can wonder?
He would not stay for me to stand and gaze.
I shook his hand and tore my heart in sunder

Light on AEH.

And went with half my life about my ways.

Darkness on Housman.
AEH is at a desk among books, inkpot and pen.
Elsewhere, simultaneously, a Selection Committee meets, comprising 'several' men. They include a Chairman, two or more speakers, designated 'Committee', and Postgate. They wear academic gowns.

AEH Am I asleep or awake? We arrive at evening upon a field of battle, where lie 200 corpses. 197 of them have no beards: the 198th has a beard on the chin; the 199th has a false beard slewed round under the left ear; the 200th has been decapitated and the head is nowhere to be found. Problem: Had it a beard, a false beard, or no beard at all? Mr Buecheler can tell you. It had a beard, a beard on the chin. I only say, look at the logic. Because a manuscript has suffered loss, therefore the lost portion contained something which Mr Buecheler wishes it to have contained: and scholars have been unable to detect any error in his reasoning.

Chairman (*reading from a letter*) 'During the last ten years, the study of the Classics has been the chief occupation of my leisure . . .'

AEH But I have long dwelt among men.

Chairman Copies of Mr Housman's testimonials are tabled.

AEH Conjectures, to Mr Marx's eyes, are arranged in a three-fold order of merit: first, the conjectures of Mr Marx; second, the conjectures of mankind in general; third, the conjectures of certain odious persons.

Committee A Post Office clerk?

Chairman Patent Office . . . supported by the Professors of Latin at Oxford and Cambridge, of Latin *and* Greek at Dublin – the editor of the *Classical Review* . . . Warren, the President of Magdalen . . .

AEH The width and variety of Francken's ignorance are wonderful. For stupidity of plan and slovenliness of execution, his *apparatus criticus* is worse than Breiter's *apparatus* to Manilius, and I never saw another of which that could be said.

Chairman (*to Postgate*) Is he well liked?

AEH Confronted with two manuscripts of equal merit, he is like a donkey between two bundles of hay, and confusedly imagines that if one bundle were removed he would cease to be a donkey.

Postgate He is . . . well remarked.

AEH The notes are vicious to a degree which well nigh protects them from refutation, so intricate is the tangle of every imaginable kind of blunder, and his main purpose in withholding useful information is to make room for a long record of conjectures which dishonour the human intellect.

Committee (*reading*) 'When Mr Housman took my Sixth Form he proved himself a thorough and sympathetic teacher . . .'

AEH Having small literary culture, he is not revolted by illiteracy or dismayed by the hideous and has a relish for the uncouth; yet would defend *pronos* against Bentley's *privos* as being very poetical, although Bentley never denied it was poetical, he only denied it was Latin.

Committee (*reading*) '. . . the sagacity and closeness desiderated by Bentley . . .' That's Warren. ' . . . one of the most interesting and attractive pupils I can remember . . .'

Chairman . . . and Robinson Ellis of Trinity . . . 'Personally I have always found Mr Housman an amiable and modest man.'

AEH No word is safe from Ellis if he can think of a similar one which is not much worse. Trying to follow his thoughts is like being in perpetual contact with an idiot child. Here is the born hater of science who fills his pages to half their height with the dregs of the Italian renaissance, and by appeals to his reader's superstition persuade him that he will gather grapes of thorns and figs of thistles.

Chairman Well . . . Professor Postgate?

Postgate Mmm.

AEH But Mr Postgate's morbid alertness is cast into deep sleep at *modo* in verse 11, and it's goodnight to grammatical science.

Committee Yes. What do *you* say, Postgate?

AEH Of Mr Postgate's '*voces*' for '*noctes*' in 33, I am at a loss to know *what* to say.

Postgate I have to declare an interest.

AEH (*continuing*) The alteration makes nonsense of the whole elegy from beginning to end.

Postgate Mr Housman is applying for this post at my urging. He is, in my view, very likely the best classical scholar in England.
    Though he is not always right on Propertius.

Chairman (*closing the meeting*) *Tempus fugit. Nunc est bibendum.*

    Light fades on Committee.

AEH When I with some thought and some pains have got this rather uninteresting garden into decent order, here is Dr Postgate hacking at the fence in a spirited attempt to re-establish chaos amongst Propertius manuscripts. All the tools he employs are two-edged, though to be sure both edges are blunt. I feel it a hardship, but I suppose it is a duty, (to) . . .

    Light on Postgate.

Postgate (*angry*) Your *stemma codicum* is fundamentally flawed – not to mince words, it is almost totally wrong. Your reliance on Baehrens's dating of the Neapolitanus was a blunder.

AEH Have you seen the paper?

Postgate I am in the act of replying to it. I intend to make you ashamed.

AEH The paper.

Postgate Oh . . .

AEH Oscar Wilde has been arrested.

Postgate Oh . . .

AEH I had no idea I had offended you, Postgate.

Postgate goes.
   Light on Stead, Labouchere and Harris with open
   newspapers. Perhaps in a railway carriage.

Stead Guilty and sentenced to two years with hard labour!

Labouchere (*reading*) 'The aesthetic cult, in its nasty form, is now over.'

Harris (*reading*) 'Open the windows! Let in the fresh air! . . . By our Dramatic Critic.'

Labouchere Convicted under the Labouchere Amendment clause!

AEH
   Oh who is that young sinner with the handcuffs on his
      wrists?
   And what has he been after that they groan and shake
      their fists?
   And wherefore is he wearing such a conscience-stricken
      air?
   Oh they're taking him to prison for the colour of his
      hair.

Harris I begged him to leave the country. I had a closed cab waiting at Hyde Park Corner and a steam-yacht at Gravesend to take him to France . . .

Labouchere (*to Stead*) Two years is totally inadequate.
   (*to Harris*) No, you didn't, Frank. You told him to brazen it out at the Café Royal.

(*to Stead*) I wanted a maximum of *seven* years.

Harris . . . With a lobster supper on board and a bottle of Pommery, and a small library of French and English books.

Labouchere Look, it wasn't a yacht, it was a table at the Café Royal.
(*to Stead*) The Attorney General of the day persuaded me that two years was more likely to secure a conviction from a hesitant jury.

Harris You did it to scupper the Bill – that's what you told me.

Labouchere Who's going to believe *you*?

Stead If Oscar Wilde's taste had been for fresh young innocent virgins of, say, sixteen, no one would have laid a finger on him.

Labouchere I did it because Stead happened to tell me just before the debate that in certain parts of London the problem of indecency between men was as serious as with virgins.

Harris There's no serious problem with virgins in certain parts of London.

Stead With virgins, there are tastes in certain parts best left to the obscurity of a learned tongue.

Harris My point.

Light fades on them.

AEH
Now 'tis oakum for his fingers and the treadmill for his
   feet
And the quarry-gang at Portland in the cold and in the
   heat,

And between his spells of labour in the time he has to
  spare
He can curse the God that made him for the colour of
  his hair.

*Three Men in a Boat row into view. Jerome has the
oars, Chamberlain (George) is trying to play a banjo.
(Frank) Harris has a first edition of* A Shropshire Lad.
  *Chamberlain, eleven years older, with a moustache,
wears a blazer striped in violent colours. Jerome and
Harris wear tweed jackets with their 'cricket trousers'.*

Chamberlain Ta-ra-ra . . . pull on your right, J. Ta-ra-ra-
boom –

Jerome Do you want to take the oars?

Chamberlain No, you're doing splendidly . . . boom-di-
ay . . .

Harris/Jerome Shut up, George!

Harris Anybody hungry?

Chamberlain Harris hasn't done any work since we left
Henley.

Harris When Chamberlain said take a boat up the river, I
understood him to mean a boat which takes passengers
from one place to another, not an arrangement where the
passengers take the boat. Personally I had no reason to
want this boat removed from where it was; as far as I
(was concerned) –

Chamberlain/Jerome Shut up, Harris!

Chamberlain Where are we, J?

Jerome Getting towards Reading.

Chamberlain Reading!

They look up-river.

Will we pass the gaol?

Jerome Perhaps Oscar will see us going by . . . he always asked for the river view at the Savoy.

Harris (*solemnly*) The prostitutes danced in the streets.

Chamberlain So did J.

Jerome I did not. It's true that as the editor of a popular newspaper I had a duty to speak out, but I take no pride in the fact that it was I as much as anybody, I suppose, who was indirectly responsible for the tragic unfolding of –

Chamberlain/Harris Shut up, J!

Jerome I'm not sorry. I might have been sorry, if he'd kept his misfortune to himself like a gentleman.

Chamberlain Posing as a gentleman.

Jerome Exactly. His work won't last either. Decadence was a blind alley in English life and letters. Wholesome humour has always been our strength. Wholesome humour and a rattling good yarn. Look at Shakespeare.

Chamberlain Or your own work.

Jerome That's not for me to say.

Chamberlain Right, Harris, take his legs.

Harris Robbie Ross gave me this man's poems. He got several off by heart to tell them to Oscar when he went to see him in prison.

Jerome Oh, yes – Gosse said to me, who is this Houseboat person Robbie likes?

Harris Not Houseboat. A. E. Housman.

Chamberlain Alfred Housman?

Harris I think he stayed with the wrong people in Shropshire. I never read such a book for telling you you're better off dead.

Chamberlain That's him!

Harris No one gets off; if you're not shot, hanged or stabbed, you kill yourself. Life's a curse, love's a blight, God's a blaggard, cherry blossom is quite nice.

Chamberlain He's a Latin prof.

Jerome But of the Greek persuasion, would you say, George?

Chamberlain Three or four years ago he was just one of us in the office.

Jerome Uranian persuasion, I mean.

Chamberlain How can one tell?

Jerome I could. Is there something eye-catching about the way he dresses?

Harris As opposed to George, you mean?

Jerome That's a point, eh, George?!

Chamberlain Pull the other one, J.

Jerome Do you want to take the oars?

The boat goes.
    AEH alone under a starry night sky. Distant bonfires. Jubilee Night, June 1897.

AEH
  'The thoughts of others
  Were light and fleeting,
  Of lovers' meeting
  Or luck or fame,

Mine were of trouble
And mine were steady,
So I was ready
When trouble came.'

*Chamberlain, at the age we saw him but in street
clothes, has joined him on the hilltop.*

Chamberlain (*simultaneous with AEH*)
'So I was ready
When trouble came.'

Pull the other one.

AEH (*pleased*) Chamberlain! I haven't thought about you
for years! You've got a moustache.

Chamberlain Hello, old chap. I'm not sure about it, but
it's growing on me.

AEH Oh, I say, that's a good one.

Chamberlain Fancy you living to a ripe old age, I
wouldn't have put a tanner on it the way you looked.

AEH When?

Chamberlain Most of the time. Happy days, I don't
think. When Jackson went off to be a headmaster in
India. No – worse before. No – worse after, when he came
home on leave to be married. No, before – that time no
one could find you for a week. I thought: the river, and no
two ways about it. But you turned up again, dry as a
stick. I did tell you, didn't I?

AEH Tell me what? Oh . . . yes, you did tell me.

Chamberlain Still, you probably wouldn't have written
the poems.

AEH This is true.

Chamberlain So it's an ill wind from yon far country blows through holt and hanger.

AEH If I might give you a piece of advice, Chamberlain, mangling a chap's poems isn't the way to show you've read them.

Chamberlain I'm word perfect. 'Oh were he and I together, shipmates on the fleeted main, sailing through the summer weather . . .' What happened to Jackson?

AEH He retired, settled in British Columbia, died of cancer.

Chamberlain Well, early though the laurel grows, it withers quicker than the rose.

AEH This is a revolting habit, Chamberlain – I forbid you.

Chamberlain Oh, I like them, I really do. Holt and hanger. Cumber. Thews. Lovely old words. Never knew what they meant. But proper poetry, no question about that. You old slyboots. You must have been writing poetry all the time you were in Trade Marks.

AEH Not so much. It was a couple of years after, something overcame me, at the beginning of '95, a ferment. I wrote half the book in the first five months of that year, before I started to calm down. It was a time of strange excitement.

Chamberlain The Oscar Wilde trials.

AEH Oh, really, Chamberlain. You should take up biography.

Chamberlain Yes, what about those ploughboys and village lads dropping like flies all over Shropshire? – those that didn't take the Queen's shilling and get shot in foreign parts.

AEH The landscape of the imagination.

Chamberlain 'Because I liked you better than suits a man to say . . .'

AEH Could you contain yourself?

Chamberlain
'But this unlucky love should last
When answered passions thin to air.'

Did you send them to Jackson, the ones you didn't put in the book?

AEH No.

Chamberlain Saving them till you're dead?

AEH It's a courtesy. Confession is an act of violence against the unoffending. Can you see the bonfires? It's the old Queen's Diamond Jubilee. I was a Victorian poet, don't forget.

Katharine joins, aged thirty-five.
Chamberlain stays.

Kate From Clee to Heaven the beacon burns!

AEH It was a grand sight. I counted fifty-two fires just to the south and west. Malvern had the biggest but it burned out in an hour.

Kate The Clent fire is a good one. The boys are here.

AEH Do I know them?

Kate Your nephews, Alfred!

AEH Oh, your boys, of course I know *them*.

Kate And the Millingtons. Mrs M. says you're no guide to Shropshire – she went to look at Hughley church and it doesn't even *have* a steeple!, never mind a graveyard full of suicides.

AEH That can surely be rectified. I never expected a two-and-six-penny book which couldn't sell out an edition of 500 copies to draw pilgrims to Hughley. I was never there, I just liked the name.

Kate Laurence thought *he* was the poet in the family, and now he knows your book by heart and recites his favourites. He met someone who told him *A Shropshire Lad* was his best yet.

AEH I hope no one is attributing *his* poems to *me*.

Kate It's sweet of him to be proud.

AEH It is, yes.

Kate We're all proud, and astonished. Clem said, 'Alfred has a heart!'

AEH No, not at all, I was depressed because of a sore throat which wouldn't leave me. I might have gone on writing poems for years, but luckily I remembered a brand of lozenges and was cured.

Kate A sore throat!?

AEH (A) punishment for a disagreeable controversy in the journals. You were clever to be a dunce, Kate, before it found you out.

Kate Oh – listen! – The larks think it's daybreak.

AEH Or the end of the world.

Kate Oh, you! Same old Alfred. (*She goes.*)

AEH But I intend to change. The day nurse will get the benefit of my transformation into 'a character', the wag of the Evelyn. I have been practising a popular style of lecture, as yet confused with memories of University College, but it's based on noticing that there are students present. I shall cause a sensation by addressing a remark to my neighbour at dinner in Hall. I am trying to think of a remark. My reputation at Trinity is for censoriousness and misanthropy. Some people say it's only shyness – impudent fools. Nevertheless, I am determined. Affability is only suffering the fools gladly, and Cambridge affords endless scope for this peculiar joy. I introduced crème brulée to Trinity, but if that isn't enough I'll talk to people. Do you still ride a bicycle?

Chamberlain Yes, a Robertson. I know your brother Laurence. We belong to a sort of secret society, the Order of Chaeronea, like the Sacred Band of Thebes. Actually it's more like a discussion group. We discuss what we should call ourselves. 'Homosexuals' has been suggested.

AEH Homosexuals?

Chamberlain We aren't anything till there's a word for it.

AEH Homosexuals? Who is responsible for this barbarity?

Chamberlain What's wrong with it?

AEH It's half Greek and half Latin!

Chamberlain That sounds about right.
What happened to me, by the way?

AEH How should I know? I suppose you became a sort of footnote. (*listening*) Listen!

The 'Marseillaise' is faintly heard.

Chamberlain The 'Marseillaise'. That's unusual, isn't it? – for the Queen's Jubilee.

AEH Oscar Wilde was in France, on the coast near Dieppe. I'd sent him my book when he came out of prison.

Darkness on Chamberlain.

The faint sound of children singing the 'Marseillaise' is overtaken by Oscar Wilde's strong fluting voice reciting.

Wilde, aged forty-one, is reading aloud from his copy of A Shropshire Lad. *He is drinking brandy, and smoking a cigarette.*

Around him is the debris of a Diamond Jubilee children's party. There is bunting, Union Jacks and Tricolours, and the remains of a large decorated cake.

Wilde
'Shot? So quick, so clean an ending?
Oh, that was right, lad, that was brave:
Yours was not an ill for mending,
T'was best to take it to the grave.'

This is not one of the ones Robbie learned for me, but your poems, when I opened your parcel, were not all strangers.

'Oh, you had forethought, you could reason,
And saw your road and where it led,
And early wise and brave in season –'

AEH To me, they're importunate friends when they take the floor.

Wilde
'And early wise and brave in season
Put the pistol to your head.'

Poor, silly boy!

AEH I read a report of the inquest in the *Evening Standard.*

Wilde Oh, thank goodness! That explains why I never believed a word of it.

AEH But it's all true.

Wilde On the contrary, it's only fact. Truth is quite another thing and is the work of the imagination.

AEH I assure you. It was not long after your trial. He was a Woolwich cadet. He blew his brains out so that he wouldn't live to shame himself, or bring shame on others. He left a letter for the coroner.

Wilde Of course he did, and you should have sent your poem to the coroner, too. Art deals with exceptions, not with types. Facts deal only with types. Here was the type of young man who shoots himself. He read about some-one shooting himself in the *Evening News*, so he shot himself in the *Evening Standard*.

AEH Oh, I say – !

Wilde
    'Oh, soon, and better so than later
    After long disgrace and scorn,
    You shot dead the household traitor,
    The soul that should not have been born.'

Still, if he hadn't shot himself before reading your poem, he would have shot himself after. I am not unfeeling. I dare say I would have wept if I'd read the newspaper. But that does not make a newspaper poetry. Art cannot be subordinate to its subject, otherwise it is not art but biography, and biography is the mesh through which our real life escapes. I was said to have walked down Piccadilly with a lily in my hand. There was no need. To do it is nothing, to be said to have done it is everything. It is the truth about me. Shakespeare's Dark Lady probably had bad breath – almost everybody did until my third year at Oxford – but sincerity is the enemy of art. This is what Pater taught me, and what Ruskin never learned. Ruskin made a vice out of virtue. Poor Pater might have made a virtue out of vice but, like your cadet, he lacked the courage to act. I breakfasted with Ruskin. Pater came to tea. The one impotent, the other terrified, they struggled for my artistic soul. But I caught syphilis from a prostitute, and the mercury cure blackened my teeth. Did we meet at Oxford?

AEH No. We once had a poem in the same magazine. Mine was for my dead mother. Yours was about the Turkish atrocities in Bulgaria.

Wilde Oh, yes, I swore never to touch Turkish champagne, and eat only Bulgarian Delight. Do you eat cake? I invited fifteen children from the village to celebrate Jubilee Day. We toasted the Queen and the President of the Republic, and the children shouted, '*Vive Monsieur Melmoth*!' I am Monsieur Melmoth. We had strawberries and chocolates and grenadine syrup, and the cake, and everyone received a present. It was one of my most successful parties. Did you come to any of my parties in London? No? But we must have had friends in common. Bernard Shaw? Frank Harris? Beardsley? Labouchere? Whistler? W. T. Stead? Did you know Henry Irving? Lily Langtry? No? The Prince of Wales? You did *have* friends?

AEH I had colleagues.

Wilde Once, I bought a huge armful of lilies in Covent Garden to give to Miss Langtry, and as I waited to put them in a cab, a small boy said to me, 'Oh, how rich you are!' . . . 'Oh, how rich you are!' (*He weeps.*) Oh – forgive me. I'm somewhat the worse for – cake. I have tried to give it up, whenever I feel myself weakening I take a glass of cognac, often I don't eat cake for days at a time; but the Jubilee broke my will, I allowed myself a social eclair out of politeness to my guests, and remember nothing more until I woke up in a welter of patisseries. Oh – Bosie! (*He weeps.*) I have to go back to him, you know. Robbie will be furious but it can't be helped. The betrayal of one's friends is a bagatelle in the stakes of love, but the betrayal of oneself is lifelong regret. Bosie is what became of me. He is spoiled, vindictive, utterly selfish and not very talented, but these are merely the facts. The truth is he was Hyacinth when Apollo loved him, he is ivory and gold, from his red rose-leaf lips comes music that fills me with joy, he is the only one who understands me. 'Even as a teething child throbs with ferment, so does the soul of him who gazes upon the boy's beauty; he can neither sleep at night nor keep still by day,' and a lot more besides, but before Plato could describe love, the loved one had to be invented. We would never love anybody if we could see past our invention. Bosie is my creation, my poem. In the mirror of invention, love discovered itself. Then we saw what we had made – the piece of ice in the fist you cannot hold or let go. (*He weeps.*) You are kind to listen.

AEH No. My life is marked by long silences. The first conjecture I ever published was on Horace. Six years later I withdrew it. Propertius I put aside nearly fifty years ago to wait for the discovery of a better manuscript, which seemed to me essential if there were the slightest hope of recovering the text. So far, silence. Meanwhile I defended the classical authors from the conjectures of idiots, and produced editions of books by Ovid, Juvenal and Lucan, and finally of Manilius, which I dedicated to my comrade Moses Jackson, and that will have to do, my sandcastle against the confounding sea. Classics apart, my life was not short enough for me to not do the things I wanted to not do, but they were few and the jackals will find it hard scavenging. I moved house four times, once, it was said, because a stranger spoke to me on my train to work. It wasn't so, but it was the truth about me. In Diamond Jubilee year I went abroad for the first time.

Wilde There's my boatman. It was he who told me you were a Latin professor, but he's profligate with titles and often confers professorships on quite unsuitable people – many of whom turn out to have chairs at our older universities.

AEH I'm very sorry. Your life is a terrible thing. A chronological error. The choice was not always between renunciation and folly. You should have lived in Megara when Theognis was writing and made his lover a song sung unto all posterity . . . and not *now*! – when disavowal and endurance are in honour, and a nameless luckless love has made notoriety your monument.

Wilde My dear fellow, a hundred francs would have done just as well. Better a fallen rocket than never a burst of light. Dante reserved a place in his Inferno for those who wilfully live in sadness – sullen in the sweet air, he says. Your 'honour' is all shame and timidity and compliance. Pure of stain! But the artist is the secret criminal in our midst. He is the agent of progress against authority. You are right to be a scholar. A scholar is all scruple, an artist is none. The artist must lie, cheat, deceive, be untrue to nature and contemptuous of history. I made my life into my art and it was an unqualified success. The blaze of my immolation threw its light into every corner of the land where uncounted young men sat each in his own darkness. What would I have done in Megara!? – think what I would have missed! I awoke the imagination of the century. I banged Ruskin's and Pater's heads together, and from the moral severity of one and the aesthetic soul of the other I made art a philosophy that can look the twentieth century in the eye. I had genius, brilliancy, daring, I took charge of my own myth. I dipped my staff into the comb of wild honey. I tasted forbidden sweetness and drank the stolen waters. I lived at the turning point of the world where everything was waking up new – the New Drama, the New Novel, New Journalism, New Hedonism, New Paganism, even the

New Woman. Where were you when all this was happening?

AEH At home.

Wilde Couldn't you at least have got a New Tailor?
Are we going together?

AEH No. I will be coming later.

Wilde You didn't mention your poems. How can you be unhappy when you know you wrote them? They are all that will still matter.

The Boatman helps Wilde aboard.

But you are not my boatman! Sebastian Melmoth *à votre service*.

Boatman Sit in the middle.

Wilde Of course.

The Boatman poles Wilde away.
    Housman is sitting on the bench by the river with a couple of books.

AEH What are you doing here, may I ask?

Housman Classics, sir.

AEH Ah.
Of course.
What year are you in now?

Housman My final year.

AEH So am I, indeed for all practical purposes I'm dead. And how are *you*? (*He picks up Housman's book.*)

Housman I'm quite well, thank you, sir.

AEH Propertius!

Housman The first of the Roman love elegists. Actually, Propertius is not set for Finals. I should be cramming, everybody expects me to get a First, you see. My family, too. I'm the eldest and I've always been . . . a scholarship boy . . . I ought to put Propertius aside now, but we're already all of us so late! – and there's someone with his Propertius coming out next year, Postgate he's called. Who knows how many of my conjectures he'll anticipate?

AEH Yes, who knows? Before you publish, by the way, the first of the Roman love elegists was not Propertius, strictly speaking. It was Cornelius Gallus.

Housman Gallus?

AEH Really and truly.

Housman But I've not read him.

AEH Nor I. Only one line of Gallus survived. The rest perished.

Housman Oh!

AEH But strictly speaking – which I do in my sleep – he was first.

Housman One line for his monument!

AEH Virgil wrote a poem for him: how much immortality does a man need? – his own poetry, all but a line, as if he had never been, but his memory alive in a garden in the northernmost province of an empire that disappeared fifteen hundred years ago. To do as much for a friend would be no small thing.

Housman Yes. (*Pause.*) Was it a good line?

AEH Quite suggestive, as it happens. I'm not sure about dead for love, though. He fought on the winning side against Antony and Cleopatra, and afterwards was put in charge of Egypt, which is not bad going for a poet. But he got above himself and was admonished by the Emperor: whereupon he killed himself. But by then he'd invented the love elegy.

Housman Propertius mentions him. 'And lately how many wounds has Gallus bathed in the waters of the Underworld, dead for love of beautiful Lycoris!' *Lately. Modo. Just recently.* They were real people to each other, that's the thing. They knew each other's poems. They knew each other's girls. Virgil puts it all in a Golden Age with pan-pipes and goatherds, and Apollo there in person – but you can trust it, that's what I mean. Real people in real love, baring their souls in poetry that made their mistresses immortal! – and it all happened in such a short span. As if all the poetry till then had to pass through a bottleneck where a handful of poets were waiting to see what could be done with it. And then it was over, the love poem complete, love as it really is.

AEH Oh, yes, there'd been songs . . . valentines – mostly in Greek, often charming . . . but the self-advertisement of farce and folly, love as abject slavery and all-out war – madness, disease, the whole catastrophe owned up to and written in the metre – no; that was new.

Housman (Oh – !)

Jackson (*off-stage*) Housman!

Pollard (*off-stage*) Housman!

Housman I'm sorry, they're calling me.

Pollard (*off-stage*) Hous! Picnic!

Jackson (*off-stage*) Locusts! Honey!

Jackson and Pollard arrive in the boat.

Housman (*to the boat*) I'm here.

AEH Mo . . .!

Pollard It's time to go.

Housman goes to the boat and gets in.

AEH I would have died for you but I never had the luck!

Housman Where are we going?

Pollard Hades.
Pull on your right, Jackson.

Jackson Do you want to take the oars?

Housman *Tendebantque manus ripae ulterioris amore.*

The boat goes.

AEH 'And they stretched out their hands in desire of the further shore.' Cleverboots was usually good for a tag. Thus Virgil, Aeneas in the Underworld, the souls of the dead reaching out across the water *ripae ulterioris amore*, you couldn't do better with a Kodak, and those who were unburied were made to wait a hundred years. I could wait a hundred if I had to. Seventy-seven go quick enough. Which is not to say I have remembered it right, messing about in a boat with Moses and dear old young Pollard on a summer's day in '79 or '80 or '81; but not impossible, not so out of court as to count as an untruth in the dream-warp of the ultimate room, though the dog is still in question. And yet not dreaming either, wide awake to all the risks – archaism, anachronism, the wayward inconsequence that only hindsight can acquit of *non sequitur*, *quietus interruptus* by monologue incontinent in the hind leg of a donkey class (you're too kind but I'm not there yet), and the unities out of the window without so much as a window to be out of: still shaky, too, from that first plummet into bathos, Greek for depth but in rhetoric a ludicrous descent from the elevated to the commonplace, as it might be from Virgil to Jerome K. Jerome if that is even a downward slope at time of speaking, and when is *that*? – for walking on water is not among my party tricks, the water and the walking work it out between them. Neither dead nor dreaming, then, but in between, not short on fact, or fiction, and suitably attired in leather boots, the very ones I was too clever for, which – here comes the fact – I left in my will to my college servant. They were too small for him but it's the thought that counts, and here is one to be going on with: In December 1894 Jerome K. Jerome, the celebrated author of *Three Men in a Boat* (*To Say Nothing of the Dog*), made an attack on an Oxford magazine, *The Chameleon* – which, he wrote, appeared to be nothing more or less than an advocacy for indulgence in the cravings of an unnatural disease. It was, he said, a case for the police. Oscar Wilde had contributed a page or two of epigrams, to oblige an Oxford student he'd befriended, Lord Alfred Douglas. Douglas himself had a poem – the one which ended 'I am the love that dare not speak its name'. Jerome's article goaded Douglas's father into leaving a card at the Albermarle Club, 'to Oscar Wilde, posing as a Sodomite'. From which all that followed, followed. Which goes to show, I know what I'm doing even when I don't know I'm doing it, in the busy hours between the tucking up and the wakey-wakey thermometer faintly antiseptic under the tongue from its dainty gauze-stoppered vase on the bedside cabinet.

Light on Jackson, then Housman.

Jackson What will become of you, Hous?

Housman
κὤτα μὲν σὺ θέλεις, μακάρεσσιν ἴσαν ἄγω
ἀμέραν· ὄτα δ' οὐκ ἐθέλησθα, μάλ' ἐν σκότῳ.

Jackson I never took to it, you know – all that *veni, vidi, vici* . . .

Housman When thou art kind I spend the day like a god; when thy face is turned aside, it is very dark with me. I shall give thee wings. Thou shalt be a song sung unto posterity so long as earth and sun abide. And when thou comest to go down to the lamentable house of Hades, never – albeit thou be dead – shalt thou lose thy fame.

Darkness on Housman and Jackson.
Dimly, Charon is seen poling Wilde across the Styx.

Wilde Wickedness is a myth invented by good people to account for the curious attractiveness of others.

One should always be a little improbable.

Nothing that actually occurs is of the smallest importance.

AEH Oxford in the Golden Age! – the hairshirts versus the Aesthetes: the neo-Christians versus the neo-pagans: the study of classics for advancement in the fair of the world versus the study of classics for the advancement of classical studies – what emotional storms, and oh what a tiny teacup. You should have been here last night when I did Hades properly – Furies, Harpies, Gorgons, and the snake-haired Medusa, to say nothing of the Dog. But now I really do have to go. How lucky to find myself standing on this empty shore, with the indifferent waters at my feet.

Fade out.